OUTRAGEOUS

Hope

EXTRAVAGANT

Joy

A STUDY IN 1 PETER

DONNA GAINES // MARGE LENOW
JEAN STOCKDALE // DAYNA STREET
ANGIE WILSON

Outrageous Hope...Extravagant Joy

# ϟ CONTENTS ϟ

# ⤜ HOW TO USE THIS STUDY ⤛

Hope and joy are not just wishful thoughts. Like the air we breathe, they are vital necessities of life—gifts that God wants to give to us. In the New Testament teachings of 1 Peter, the old fisherman gives practical instructions on how to live energized by the Spirit, no matter what. *Outrageous Hope—Extravagant Joy* is a ten-week study in 1 Peter, a God-breathed letter that will challenge us to realize life, not a futile, empty way of living (1 Peter 1:18), but real life, the Christ-life.

This study is designed to provide an opportunity for personal study throughout the week leading up to a small group discussion and large group teaching time once a week. Each session is divided into five daily homework assignments that provide Bible study and personal application.

In your small group time each week, you will be able to connect with other women and build life-giving, sharpening relationships. As you meet together, be ready to share what God has shown you through His Word using the weekly studies as a guide. In the large group teaching time, you will be challenged by relevant, biblical instruction that will encourage you to embrace life with Outrageous Hope and Extravagant Joy!

# THE FIRST LETTER OF PETER

## (NASB)

**1** Peter, an apostle of Jesus Christ, To those who reside as aliens, scattered throughout Pontus, Galatia, Cappadocia, Asia, and Bithynia, who are chosen [2] according to the foreknowledge of God the Father, by the sanctifying work of the Spirit, to obey Jesus Christ and be sprinkled with His blood: May grace and peace be yours in the fullest measure.

[3] Blessed be the God and Father of our Lord Jesus Christ, who according to His great mercy has caused us to be born again to a living hope through the resurrection of Jesus Christ from the dead, [4] to *obtain* an inheritance *which is* imperishable and undefiled and will not fade away, reserved in heaven for you, [5] who are protected by the power of God through faith for a salvation ready to be revealed in the last time. [6] In this you greatly rejoice, even though now for a little while, if necessary, you have been distressed by various trials, [7] so that the proof of your faith, *being* more precious than gold which is perishable, even though tested by fire, may be found to result in praise and glory and honor at the revelation of Jesus Christ; [8] and though you have not seen Him, you love Him, and though you do not see Him now, but believe in Him, you greatly rejoice with joy inexpressible and full of glory, [9] obtaining as the outcome of your faith the salvation of your souls.

[10] As to this salvation, the prophets who prophesied of the grace that *would come* to you made careful searches and inquiries, [11] seeking to know what person or time the Spirit of Christ within them was indicating as He predicted the sufferings of Christ and the glories to follow. [12] It was revealed to them that they were not serving themselves, but you, in these things which now have been announced to you through those who preached the gospel to you by the Holy Spirit sent from heaven—things into which angels long to look.

[13] Therefore, prepare your minds for action, keep sober *in spirit*, fix your hope completely on the grace to be brought to you at the revelation of Jesus Christ. [14] As obedient children, do not be conformed to the former lusts *which were yours* in your ignorance, [15] but like the Holy One who called you, be holy yourselves also in all *your* behavior; [16] because it is written, "You shall be holy, for I am holy."

[17] If you address as Father the One who impartially judges according to each one's work, conduct yourselves in fear during the time of your stay *on earth*; [18] knowing that you were not redeemed with perishable things like silver or gold from your futile way of life inherited from your forefathers, [19] but with precious blood, as of a lamb unblemished and spotless, *the blood* of Christ. [20] For He was foreknown before the foundation of the world, but has appeared in these last times for the sake of you [21] who through Him are believers in God, who raised Him from the dead and gave Him glory, so that your faith and hope are in God.

²² Since you have in obedience to the truth purified your souls for a sincere love of the brethren, fervently love one another from the heart, ²³ for you have been born again not of seed which is perishable but imperishable, *that is*, through the living and enduring word of God. ²⁴ For,

"All flesh is like grass,
And all its glory like the flower of grass.
The grass withers,
And the flower falls off,
²⁵ But the word of the Lord endures forever."

And this is the word which was preached to you.

**2** Therefore, putting aside all malice and all deceit and hypocrisy and envy and all slander, ² like newborn babies, long for the pure milk of the word, so that by it you may grow in respect to salvation, ³ if you have tasted the kindness of the Lord.

⁴ And coming to Him as to a living stone which has been rejected by men, but is choice and precious in the sight of God, ⁵ you also, as living stones, are being built up as a spiritual house for a holy priesthood, to offer up spiritual sacrifices acceptable to God through Jesus Christ. ⁶ For *this* is contained in Scripture:

"Behold, I lay in Zion a choice stone, a precious corner *stone*,
And he who believes in Him will not be disappointed."

⁷ This precious value, then, is for you who believe; but for those who disbelieve,

"The stone which the builders rejected,
This became the very corner *stone*,"

⁸ and, "A stone of stumbling and a rock of offense";

for they stumble because they are disobedient to the word, and
to this *doom* they were also appointed.

⁹ But you are a chosen race, a royal priesthood, a holy nation, a people for *God's* own possession, so that you may proclaim the excellencies of Him who has called you out of darkness into His marvelous light; ¹⁰ for you once were not a people, but now you are the people of God; you had not received mercy, but now you have received mercy. ¹¹ Beloved, I urge you as aliens and strangers to abstain from fleshly lusts which wage war against the soul. ¹² Keep your behavior excellent among the Gentiles, so that in the thing in which they slander you as evildoers, they may because of your good deeds, as they observe *them*, glorify God in the day of visitation.

¹³ Submit yourselves for the Lord's sake to every human institution, whether to a king as the one in authority, ¹⁴ or to governors as sent by him for the punishment of evildoers and the praise of those

who do right. ¹⁵ For such is the will of God that by doing right you may silence the ignorance of foolish men. ¹⁶ *Act* as free men, and do not use your freedom as a covering for evil, but *use it* as bondslaves of God. ¹⁷ Honor all people, love the brotherhood, fear God, honor the king. ¹⁸ Servants, be submissive to your masters with all respect, not only to those who are good and gentle, but also to those who are unreasonable. ¹⁹ For this *finds* favor, if for the sake of conscience toward God a person bears up under sorrows when suffering unjustly. ²⁰ For what credit is there if, when you sin and are harshly treated, you endure it with patience? But if when you do what is right and suffer *for it* you patiently endure it, this *finds* favor with God.

²¹ For you have been called for this purpose, since Christ also suffered for you, leaving you an example for you to follow in His steps, ²² who committed no sin, nor was any deceit found in His mouth; ²³ and while being reviled, He did not revile in return; while suffering, He uttered no threats, but kept entrusting *Himself* to Him who judges righteously; ²⁴ and He Himself bore our sins in His body on the cross, so that we might die to sin and live to righteousness; for by His wounds you were healed. ²⁵ For you were continually straying like sheep, but now you have returned to the Shepherd and Guardian of your souls.

**3** In the same way, you wives, be submissive to your own husbands so that even if any *of them* are disobedient to the word, they may be won without a word by the behavior of their wives, ² as they observe your chaste and respectful behavior. ³ Your adornment must not be *merely* external—braiding the hair, and wearing gold jewelry, or putting on dresses; ⁴ but *let it be* the hidden person of the heart, with the imperishable quality of a gentle and quiet spirit, which is precious in the sight of God. ⁵ For in this way in former times the holy women also, who hoped in God, used to adorn themselves, being submissive to their own husbands; ⁶ just as Sarah obeyed Abraham, calling him lord, and you have become her children if you do what is right without being frightened by any fear.

⁷ You husbands in the same way, live with *your wives* in an understanding way, as with someone weaker, since she is a woman; and show her honor as a fellow heir of the grace of life, so that your prayers will not be hindered.

⁸ To sum up, all of you be harmonious, sympathetic, brotherly, kindhearted, and humble in spirit; ⁹ not returning evil for evil or insult for insult, but giving a blessing instead; for you were called for the very purpose that you might inherit a blessing. ¹⁰ For,

"The one who desires life, to love and see good days,
Must keep his tongue from evil and his lips from speaking deceit.
¹¹ "He must turn away from evil and do good;
He must seek peace and pursue it.
¹² "For the eyes of the Lord are toward the righteous,
And His ears attend to their prayer,

But the face of the Lord is against those who do evil."

¹³ Who is there to harm you if you prove zealous for what is good? ¹⁴ But even if you should suffer for the sake of righteousness, you are blessed. And do not fear their intimidation, and do not be troubled, ¹⁵ but sanctify Christ as Lord in your hearts, always *being* ready to make a defense to everyone who asks you to give an account for the hope that is in you, yet with gentleness and reverence; ¹⁶ and keep a good conscience so that in the thing in which you are slandered, those who revile your good behavior in Christ will be put to shame. ¹⁷ For it is better, if God should will it so, that you suffer for doing what is right rather than for doing what is wrong.

¹⁸ For Christ also died for sins once for all, *the* just for *the* unjust, so that He might bring us to God, having been put to death in the flesh, but made alive in the spirit; ¹⁹ in which also He went and made proclamation to the spirits *now* in prison, ²⁰ who once were disobedient, when the patience of God kept waiting in the days of Noah, during the construction of the ark, in which a few, that is, eight persons, were brought safely through *the* water. ²¹ Corresponding to that, baptism now saves you—not the removal of dirt from the flesh, but an appeal to God for a good conscience—through the resurrection of Jesus Christ, ²² who is at the right hand of God, having gone into heaven, after angels and authorities and powers had been subjected to Him.

**4** Therefore, since Christ has suffered in the flesh, arm yourselves also with the same purpose, because he who has suffered in the flesh has ceased from sin, ² so as to live the rest of the time in the flesh no longer for the lusts of men, but for the will of God. ³ For the time already past is sufficient *for you* to have carried out the desire of the Gentiles, having pursued a course of sensuality, lusts, drunkenness, carousing, drinking parties and abominable idolatries. ⁴ In *all* this, they are surprised that you do not run with *them* into the same excesses of dissipation, and they malign *you*; ⁵ but they will give account to Him who is ready to judge the living and the dead. ⁶ For the gospel has for this purpose been preached even to those who are dead, that though they are judged in the flesh as men, they may live in the spirit according to *the will of* God.

⁷ The end of all things is near; therefore, be of sound judgment and sober *spirit* for the purpose of prayer. ⁸ Above all, keep fervent in your love for one another, because love covers a multitude of sins. ⁹ Be hospitable to one another without complaint. ¹⁰ As each one has received a *special* gift, employ it in serving one another as good stewards of the manifold grace of God. ¹¹ Whoever speaks, *is to do so* as one who is speaking the utterances of God; whoever serves *is to do so* as one who is serving by the strength which God supplies; so that in all things God may be glorified through Jesus Christ, to whom belongs the glory and dominion forever and ever. Amen.

¹² Beloved, do not be surprised at the fiery ordeal among you, which comes upon you for your testing, as though some strange thing were happening to you; ¹³ but to the degree that you share the sufferings of Christ, keep on rejoicing, so that also at the revelation of His glory you may rejoice with exultation. ¹⁴ If

you are reviled for the name of Christ, you are blessed, because the Spirit of glory and of God rests on you. ¹⁵ Make sure that none of you suffers as a murderer, or thief, or evildoer, or a troublesome meddler; ¹⁶ but if *anyone suffers* as a Christian, he is not to be ashamed, but is to glorify God in this name. ¹⁷ For *it is* time for judgment to begin with the household of God; and if *it begins* with us first, what *will be* the outcome for those who do not obey the gospel of God? ¹⁸ And if it is with difficulty that the righteous is saved, what will become of the godless man and the sinner? ¹⁹ Therefore, those also who suffer according to the will of God shall entrust their souls to a faithful Creator in doing what is right.

**5** Therefore, I exhort the elders among you, as *your* fellow elder and witness of the sufferings of Christ, and a partaker also of the glory that is to be revealed, ² shepherd the flock of God among you, exercising oversight not under compulsion, but voluntarily, according to *the will of* God; and not for sordid gain, but with eagerness; ³ nor yet as lording it over those allotted to your charge, but proving to be examples to the flock. ⁴ And when the Chief Shepherd appears, you will receive the unfading crown of glory. ⁵ You younger men, likewise, be subject to *your* elders; and all of you, clothe yourselves with humility toward one another, for God is opposed to the proud, but gives grace to the humble.

⁶ Therefore humble yourselves under the mighty hand of God, that He may exalt you at the proper time, ⁷ casting all your anxiety on Him, because He cares for you. ⁸ Be of sober *spirit*, be on the alert. Your adversary, the devil, prowls around like a roaring lion, seeking someone to devour. ⁹ But resist him, firm in *your* faith, knowing that the same experiences of suffering are being accomplished by your brethren who are in the world. ¹⁰ After you have suffered for a little while, the God of all grace, who called you to His eternal glory in Christ, will Himself perfect, confirm, strengthen *and* establish you. ¹¹ To Him *be* dominion forever and ever. Amen.

¹² Through Silvanus, our faithful brother (for so I regard *him*), I have written to you briefly, exhorting and testifying that this is the true grace of God. Stand firm in it! ¹³ She who is in Babylon, chosen together with you, sends you greetings, and *so does* my son, Mark. ¹⁴ Greet one another with a kiss of love.

Peace be to you all who are in Christ.

# OUTRAGEOUS HOPE...EXTRAVAGANT JOY
## Introduction

*So that the proof of your faith, being more precious than gold which is perishable, even though tested by fire, may be found to result in praise and glory and honor at the revelation of Jesus Christ...* 1 Peter 1:7

*Fight for us, O God, that we not drift numb and blind and foolish into vain and empty excitements. Life is too short, too precious, too painful to waste on worldly bubbles that burst. Heaven is too great, hell is too horrible, eternity is too long that we should putter around on the porch of eternity.*[1]
~ John Piper

The 2004 presidential election in Ukraine is considered the most significant event in the country since it achieved its independence after the dissolution of the Soviet Union in 1991. Viktor Yushchenko ran on a pro-democracy platform that supported integration into the Euro-Atlantic community challenging the more authoritarian ruling party that wanted to maintain the status-quo. During the campaign, Yushchenko almost died from a mysterious case of dioxin poisoning that permanently disfigured his face. But that would not keep him from pressing forward. On the day of the election, exit polls showed Yushchenko in the lead by 10 percent. In an effort to tamper with the results, the state-run television station, controlled by the ruling party, reported that Yushchenko had been defeated. It seemed that all hope for a new Ukraine had disappeared.

However, in the lower right-hand corner of the television screen a courageous woman by the name of Natalia Dmitruk was signing the broadcast for the deaf community. As the newsperson repeated the doctored results from the ruling party, Dmitruk refused to translate them. Instead she signed, "I am addressing everybody who is deaf in Ukraine. Our president is Viktor Yushchenko. Do not trust the results of the central election committee. They are all lies...And I am very ashamed to translate such lies to you."[2]

The deaf community sprang into action. They began to send text messages about the fraudulent results being reported and as the news of Dmitruk's solo act of defiance spread, hundreds of journalists were moved to follow her lead and tell the truth. Over the next few weeks, the "Orange Revolution"

"Don't believe the big screen" is the lyric of hope laced throughout Scripture. The world, the flesh, and the devil shout discouragement and defeat on the big screen while in the lower right hand corner, Jesus beckons us to follow Him and embrace a life of outrageous hope and extravagant joy.

ensued as a million people wearing orange marched to the capital city of Kiev demanding a new election. The government was forced to concede and hold a new election; Viktor Yushchenko became president.

Reflecting on this historic turn of events, Philip Yancey writes:

When I heard the story behind the orange revolution, the image of a small screen of truth in the corner of the big screen became for me an ideal picture of the church. You see we as a church do not control the big screen. (When we do, we usually mess it up.) Go to any magazine rack or turn on the television and you see a consistent message. What matters is how beautiful you are, how much money or power you have. Similarly, though the world includes many poor people, they rarely make the magazine covers or the news shows. Instead we focus on the superrich, names like Bill Gates or Oprah Winfrey…Our society is hardly unique. Throughout history nations have always glorified winners, not losers. Then, like the sign language translator in the lower right-hand corner of the screen, along comes a person named Jesus who says in effect, *Don't believe the big screen – they're lying. It's the poor who are blessed, not the rich. Mourners are blessed too, as well as those who hunger and thirst, and the persecuted. Those who go through life thinking they're on top end up on the bottom. And those who go through life feeling they're on the bottom end up on the top. After all, what does it profit a person to gain the whole world and lose his soul?* [3]

"Don't believe the big screen" is the lyric of hope laced throughout Scripture. The world, the flesh, and the devil shout discouragement and defeat on the big screen while in the lower right hand corner, Jesus beckons us to follow Him and embrace a life of outrageous hope and extravagant joy.

Such was the call He issued to Peter, the strong-willed and courageous man's man who never did anything halfway. He was a determined fisherman, a loyal friend, and a zealous disciple, that is until he failed miserably when he denied the Lord not once, not twice, but three times. That failure, along with the subsequent death of Jesus, were crippling to Peter. Hope. Was. Gone. And then on the third day, after what was most certainly the worst day of his life, an angel appeared to the women who had gone to the tomb telling them that Jesus had risen and to "go tell his disciples **and Peter**…"(Mark 16:7, bold print mine).

Charles Swindoll writes that those two words, "and Peter" reintroduced hope back "into the fisherman's life...the one ingredient without which he could otherwise not recover. Upon hearing of his Savior's resurrection and also his Savior's concern that *he* especially be given the message, Peter had hope beyond his failure. Because of that he could go on."[4]

So it is not surprising that Peter is the one who would write a letter of hope entwined with joy to the "aliens, scattered" across the vast Roman Empire who needed a reminder of the glorious inheritance that was theirs through Christ. Like most letters, 1 Peter has a sender, recipients, and a postmark. Those elements will paint the backdrop for the contrarian message of the small screen contained in the letter, a message that will never fade away.

# THE SENDER

Peter was an eyewitness to the majesty of Christ. He saw first-hand the Savior's life, His death, His resurrection, His ascension. And as Peter penned his first letter, he wrote from the vantage of that personal account. In the years between his cataclysmic failure and the writing of this letter, the fisherman turned disciple was filled with the Holy Spirit at Pentecost and subsequently used as a catalyst for spiritual awakening in Jerusalem and beyond. And the results were amazing, with the first half of the book of Acts detailing Peter's ministry as he leads the early church in spreading the Gospel throughout Judea, Galilee, and Samaria (Acts 9:31), resulting in many "signs and wonders" (Acts 5:12), and thousands upon thousands being reached for Christ.

What is immediately noticeable in the letter is the imprint of brokenness and grace on Peter's life. Gone is the brash, reactive, let's fix the problem by cutting off an ear Peter. It is not that he has lost his passion; it is that his passion has been transformed. And what has emerged from the humiliation of failure is the humility of a caring shepherd who longs to gently lift the heads of fellow believers to see beyond their circumstances and suffering to the living hope they have in Jesus Christ.

# THE RECIPIENTS

Peter's opening salutation greeted believers who had been driven from their homes and were now scattered throughout the countries of Pontus, Galatia, Cappadocia, Asia, and Bithynia (modern Turkey). These Jewish and Gentile believers had been separated from their families and were living as aliens in foreign lands. And as if it was not difficult enough to live as strangers, without any of the rights that accompany citizenship, they had become targets of political and religious persecution.

Much of Rome was destroyed by fire in AD 64. Nero, the deranged emperor, had an insatiable lust to build and thus was the prime suspect for the arson. In order to deflect suspicion from himself, he blamed Christians for the fire and viciously persecuted them.

Warren Wiersbe notes:

> The important thing for us to know about these "scattered strangers" is that they were going through a time of suffering and persecution. At least fifteen times in this letter Peter referred to suffering, and he used eight different Greek words to do so. Some of these Christians were suffering because they were living godly lives and doing what was good and right...Others were suffering reproach for the name of Christ...and being railed at by unsaved people...Peter wrote to encourage them to be good witnesses to their persecutors, and to remember that their suffering would lead to glory.[5]

Suffering, hostility, and persecution were daily realities for the believers who received Peter's letter. Shallow words of sympathy would have melted in the heat of the dire circumstances they faced. Instead, Peter gives them practical instructions on how to conduct themselves as the people of God in the times in which they lived and to claim the "living hope" that was theirs through the living Lord and His "living and enduring Word."

# THE POSTMARK

The postmark provides both the place and date of a letter's posting. At the time 1 Peter is written, Peter had not yet been arrested, an event that would culminate with his martyrdom around AD 66–68. However, the persecution of Christians was already underway so most theologians believe that Peter's first letter was written in AD 64-65, after Rome was set ablaze in July AD 64.

In 1 Peter 5:13, Peter sends greetings from the local church, calling it "Babylon". But since it is unlikely that Peter, Mark, and Silvanus were all at the small distant location in Mesopotamia at the same time, it is more likely that "Babylon" is an alias for Rome, the modern city that followed the idolatrous example of ancient Babylon. To protect the church in Rome from further tyrannical persecution, it is probable that Peter used "Babylon" as a code word for the imperial city.

# THE MESSAGE

*Joy* is not contingent upon circumstance. *Hope* is not tied to the news of the day.

Throughout Peter's letter he urgently persuades his readers, "Don't believe the big screen." Joy is not contingent upon circumstance. Hope is not tied to the news of the day.

*Your life is a journey you must travel with a deep consciousness of God. It cost God plenty to get you out of that dead-end, empty-headed life you grew up in. He paid with Christ's sacred blood, you know. He died like an unblemished, sacrificial lamb. And this was no afterthought. Even though it has only lately—at the end of the ages—become public knowledge, God always knew he was going to do this for you. It's because of this sacrificed Messiah, whom God then raised from the dead and glorified, that you trust God, that you know you have a future in God (1 Peter 1:18-21, MSG).*

The words that are close to 2000 years old remain as relevant today. As we immerse ourselves in this God-breathed letter written by an old fisherman, I pray the ink from Peter's pen will leave a lasting impression on our lives. And as a result, may we be people of the "small screen" who refuse to *putter around on the porch of eternity* but courageously stand for Truth and live each day of our remaining years with **Outrageous Hope and Extravagant Joy!**

# 1 PETER TIMELINE
## (approximate)

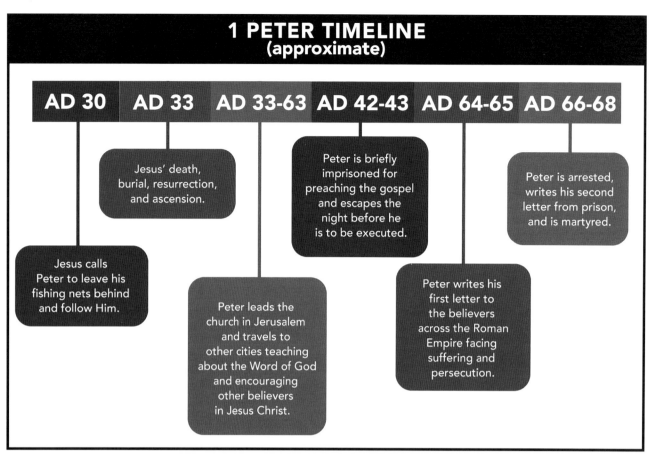

| AD 30 | AD 33 | AD 33-63 | AD 42-43 | AD 64-65 | AD 66-68 |

Jesus' death, burial, resurrection, and ascension.

Peter is briefly imprisoned for preaching the gospel and escapes the night before he is to be executed.

Peter is arrested, writes his second letter from prison, and is martyred.

Jesus calls Peter to leave his fishing nets behind and follow Him.

Peter leads the church in Jerusalem and travels to other cities teaching about the Word of God and encouraging other believers in Jesus Christ.

Peter writes his first letter to the believers across the Roman Empire facing suffering and persecution.

# WHERE EVENTS IN 1 PETER HAPPENED

Black Sea

Adriatic Sea

Rome

ITALY

Philippi

BITHYNIA

PONTUS

GALATIA

Aegean Sea

ASIA

CAPPADOCIA

ACHAIA

Corinth

Ephesus

Antioch

SYRIA

Cyrene

Mediterranean Sea

Caesarea

Joppa

Sebaste

Alexandria

Lydda

Jerusalem

0    250    500
km

# WEEK 1

## Because He Lives

### 1 PETER 1:1-12

*Blessed be the God and Father of our Lord Jesus Christ, who according to His great mercy has caused us to be born again to a living hope through the resurrection of Jesus Christ from the dead, to obtain an inheritance which is imperishable and undefiled and will not fade away, reserved in Heaven for you.*

1 Peter 1:3-4

*True Christian hope is more than "hope so." It is confident assurance of future glory and blessing.* [6]

~ Warren Wiersbe

Though centuries have passed since the content of this letter was conceptualized by the Apostle Peter through the inspiration of the Holy Spirit, the message remains applicable and fresh in the turbulent world in which we live. Like the original recipients, we find ourselves in a world that is becoming increasingly intolerant toward Christianity. Yet it is not so different from the experience of the New Testament church. Can't you just see the Apostle Peter reminiscing about what the Lord Jesus told the disciples about their relationship with the world? "If the world hates you, you know that it has hated Me before it hated you. If you were of the world, the world would love its own; but because you are not of the world, but I chose you out of the world, because of this the world hates you" (John 15:18-19).

Peter had walked with the Lord Himself and was approaching the end of his life. He understood the sustaining power of the gift of salvation and the hope it engendered in the life of the believer. He is compelled to tell them that while persecution would come, they had an inheritance secure in Heaven. What an encouragement this letter must have been in a culture where the tide was turning against them! No doubt this letter has ministered to Christians down through the centuries and has a tender message from the Apostle Peter for us as well. So, let's plunge right in. We will begin our study with some background research on the writer of the letter, Peter.

# ⇒ WEEK 1 · DAY ONE ⇐

When the name Peter is mentioned, my mind immediately goes to the most famous Peter of all time, the Apostle Peter. A little smile then forms on my lips as I think of this bigger-than-life disciple of Jesus Christ. The New Testament narrative gives us many glimpses into his life and ministry with the portrayal of his keen spiritual insights juxtaposed with his impetuous nature and eventual denial of Jesus. Despite this failure, Peter, one of three in Jesus' inner circle, rose from defeat to be used powerfully in the development of the church. Peter's teaching in 1 Peter is based on his life experience with Jesus Christ. Today, we will trace his growth as he progresses into the authoritative leader of the apostles and the spokesman for the church by reviewing passages from pertinent Scriptures. Be sure to include any insights you glean about Peter or Jesus as you answer the questions.

1.  Read John 1:40-42 and Matthew 4:18-22. How did Peter meet Jesus and what was the direct result?

    Jesus calls to peter + his brother to follow Him. They drop their nets and just that. Jesus calls them to be "fishers of men"

2.  Using Matthew 14:26-33 as a reference, what was Peter's response to Jesus walking on the water?

    he questioned whether it was truly Jesus and tested him by saying if it is truly you call me to walk on water to you. Jesus does just that and peter sinks as he doubts calling to Jesus for help.

3.  What was Peter's declaration following Jesus' question in Matthew 16:13-17?

    Jesus is christ the son of the living God

4.  How was Peter's opinion substantiated in Matthew 17:1-8?

5.  What did Peter do upon the arrest of Jesus (Matthew 26:69-75)?

6.  What was Jesus' response to Peter after His resurrection and how did it impact his life (John 21:15-17)?

7.  As you consider the transformation in Peter's life, chronicle how the surety of forgiveness and the blessing of salvation has changed your life.

Let's fast forward to the day of Pentecost where we see a transformed Apostle Peter fearlessly preaching the gospel. Gone was his hesitancy to identify with Jesus Christ. After all, he had been forgiven and commissioned by his Lord. He had a message to proclaim.

8.  Read Peter's Pentecost message as recorded in Acts 2:14-41. Make a list of the key doctrines of Christianity that you find in this passage.

The response to Peter's persuasive sermon was phenomenal—about three thousand people responded to his message in faith and the New Testament church was birthed. If you follow the Biblical narrative through the first fifteen chapters of Acts, you will see Peter courageously preaching the gospel, performing miracles, and leading the church despite threats and arrests. Then suddenly, Scripture is silent about his activities aside from mention of him by Paul in his letters which record that Peter was actively involved in the life of the church and missionary endeavors. When turmoil began to kindle in the Roman Empire, we hear from Peter again in his letters of encouragement to the believers in Asia Minor. Tradition holds that Peter was martyred soon after he penned the two letters – crucified upside down. Yet, his influence and encouragement live on. Praise the Lord for His life-changing Word!

We can approach our initial study in the book of 1 Peter today with great anticipation. The one who walked with Jesus has a message for us.

Read 1 Peter 1:1-2.

Peter began his letter with the customary salutation commencing with his name. He then added "an apostle of Jesus Christ." Without question, these believers would have had no difficulty identifying one of Jesus' original disciples, so Peter undoubtedly was reminding them of his apostolic authority. Thomas Schreiner defines the significance of this descriptive phrase well:

> The opening greeting in 1 Peter is hardly a customary hello. It is theologically rich and densely packed with themes. The author, Peter, introduces himself as an apostle of Jesus Christ. He does not mean by this merely that he is a messenger of Christ. The word "apostle" is used in the technical sense. Jesus Christ designated Peter as an authoritative messenger and interpreter of the gospel. The letter does not represent good advice but a binding apostolic word for the church. [7]

The office of apostle was very influential in the early church and was reserved for those who met certain standards.

1.  Read Acts 1:21-24 and 1 Corinthians 12:28. What requirements were essential for apostleship?

2. Based on the information you discovered in the previous question, do you think the office of apostle in the church was temporary or on-going? Why?

Once Peter establishes his apostolic authority, he categorizes the recipients of the letter.

3. How are the recipients of Peter's letter identified in verse one? Where did they live?

The destination for Peter's letter was Asia Minor, now modern-day Turkey. Following the martyrdom of Stephen, persecution broke out in Jerusalem, and many believers migrated to other locations where they proclaimed the gospel. This circular letter was to be delivered to the churches in five provinces, probably in the order in which they were listed. Peter refers to these believers as strangers or aliens who were scattered about Asia Minor. Many had left their homes because of persecution and were sojourners in a strange land. Yet, as Christians, we can also feel like strangers in a land unfamiliar to us.

4. Do you ever feel like a stranger in the world? In what way?

5. Based on Philippians 3:20, where is a Christian's citizenship?

In *the Bible Knowledge Commentary: An Exposition of the Scriptures*, R.M. Raymer notes: "Christians, whose citizenship is in Heaven, live in the midst of a pagan society as aliens and sojourners, displaced persons whose thoughts should often turn toward their true home." [8] Indeed, this world does not feel like home for us today nor did it for those first century Christians. Our values and worldview are decidedly different for our citizenship is in Heaven. We are not comfortable here because, quite frankly; it's just not home.

After Peter acknowledges the believers' geographical location, he then recognizes their spiritual designation. They were the elect, the chosen of God.

> Indeed, this world does not feel like home for us today nor did it for those first century Christians. Our *values* and *worldview* are decidedly different for our citizenship is in *Heaven*. We are not comfortable here because, quite frankly; it's just not home.

6. What three ministries of the Godhead does Peter outline in his explanation of salvation in 1 Peter 1:1-2?

What a beautiful picture of the interworking of the Trinity to provide salvation for mankind! The Holy Spirit sets us apart for obedience to Jesus Christ, the Son, Who has sprinkled us with His blood to provide the propitiation (atoning sacrifice) for our sins. Warren Wiersbe sums it up like this: "We have been chosen by the Father, purchased by the Son, and set apart by the Spirit. It takes all three if there is to be a true experience of salvation." [9]

This picture of the sprinkling of blood refers back to the Old Testament establishment of the covenant between God and the Children of Israel.

7. Read Exodus 24:1-8. What did Moses do with the blood of the sacrifices and what did his action signify?

8. According to Hebrews 12:24, what was required for the establishment of the New Covenant?

Dr. Mark Castellaw, a member of Bellevue Baptist Church, frequently lectures on the crucifixion of Jesus from the perspective of a medical doctor. Recently, he shared this insight regarding His sacrificial death.

All of us one day will have a death certificate with our name on it and the cause of death. If Jesus would have had a death certificate, what would it have said?

Jesus of Nazareth died this day of the following causes:

1. Massive blood loss due to severe lacerations of torso and head
2. Massive blunt trauma to chest and body
3. Severe dehydration
4. Pulmonary edema and effusions
5. Pericardial effusion and tamponade
6. Cardiac rupture (or a broken heart)
7. Hypoxia and suffocation
8. My sin and your sin (Put your name here.)

According to Dr. Castellaw, the last item on the death certificate is the official cause of death. The other elements listed signify the scope of His suffering as Jesus sprinkled His blood for my sin and yours.

Peter closed his salutation with a blessing of grace and peace for the believers in Asia Minor. How appropriate – for it was through grace (God's riches at Christ's expense) that those believers could rest in peace despite any persecution that came their way. Their home was in Heaven.

Grace and peace to you, my fellow sojourner.

In his salutation to the believers in Asia Minor, Peter reminds them of the work of the Trinity in their salvation—God the Father who chose them, the Holy Spirit who set them apart and sanctified them, and Jesus Christ who through His death sprinkled His blood on the mercy seat on their behalf. Peter, showing his heart for instruction as a spiritual father, then transitions into a litany of praise to God the Father and modeled what gratefulness and praise looked like in light of so great a salvation. They were the recipients of God's great mercy. That was reason to rejoice! Likewise, ladies, may our hearts overflow with praise as we examine 1 Peter 1:3-5 today. Let the doxology begin!

1. Read 1 Peter 1:3-5. Make a list of all the blessings and promises you discover as you read today's passage.

This passage is full of Biblical truth that should cause us to rejoice from the very depth of our souls. Let's take a few moments to look deeper into these doctrinal concepts. Peter reminds the believers that they had been born again. No doubt he was reflecting on the conversation between Jesus and Nicodemus when Jesus said, "Truly, truly, I say to you, unless one is born again he cannot see the kingdom of God" (John 3:3). Of course, the new birth Jesus refers to was the salvation He would provide by His death and resurrection.

2. What is the source of our rich salvation according to verse 3?

The Greek word *eleos* is translated as mercy, compassion, pity. It instills the idea of unmerited favor or giving to one what one does not deserve. Though so unworthy of God's gift of mercy, we are the recipients of its benefits.

3.  Investigate the following verses and record the characteristics of God's mercy that you find.

Ephesians 2:4

Psalm 86:5

Psalm 103:8

Psalm 106:1

Lamentations 3:22-23

4. What does Peter say the believer receives as a natural consequence when he or she is born again? (v.3)

Adrian Rogers, former pastor of Bellevue Baptist Church, frequently reminded believers that theirs was a "know so" salvation rather than a "hope so" salvation. Our *hope* is alive and secure because it rests in the *living* Jesus Christ whom we can confidently trust to provide the salvation He has promised.

In today's vernacular, hope expresses a desire that something will happen. But in the spiritual sense, hope has the ring of absolute assurance for the believer. Adrian Rogers, former pastor of Bellevue Baptist Church, frequently reminded believers that theirs was a "know so" salvation rather than a "hope so" salvation. Our hope is alive and secure because it rests in the living Jesus Christ whom we can confidently trust to provide the salvation He has promised. Warren Wiersbe gives some insight concerning the Christian's hope: "Time destroys most hopes; they fade and then die. But the passing of time only makes a Christian's hope that much more glorious." [10]

5.  What was necessary for God's gift of salvation to be accomplished? (v.3)

Christ's resurrection from the dead is a key component in the understanding of salvation. Without the resurrection, Christ did not conquer death and the believer has no hope for eternal life. The ESV Study Bible relates: "The resurrection is not merely a doctrine to be affirmed intellectually, it is the resounding affirmation that Jesus reigns over all, and the power that raised him from the dead is the Christian's power for living the Christian life on earth and the assurance of eternal life in heaven." [11] We have a living hope because He is alive!

6.  Read 1 Peter 1:4. What other blessing does the believer receive because of salvation?

7.  Define the descriptive words Peter uses in verse 4 to describe this blessing. Use a dictionary if you like.

Upon the entrance of sin into God's perfect creation, the decay began. What had once been unmarred, permanent, and unfading became fleeting. No doubt you have noticed the phenomenon. Recently, my mother laughingly told the story of finding a long-abandoned swimsuit in a drawer. When she picked it up to remove it, it merely crumbled in her fingers. Consider also the deterioration of our physical bodies. Right now, I imagine you are thinking, "Must we?" A glimpse at a picture from fifteen years ago will report the truth. While visiting us this week, my young grandson remarked while holding my hand, "Mimi, I love the wrinkled skin on your hands." Bless his sweet heart. That might not have been my response, but it is refreshing to see my wrinkled hands through the eyes of love. In God's domain, our inheritance remains imperishable, undefiled, and unfading. The decay of sin cannot reach it.

8.  Review verses 4-5. Upon what does the security of the believer and our inheritance rest?

9.  What response does this revelation rouse within you?

What a rich study we have had today! We can rejoice that we have been born again into a living hope. An eternal inheritance is ours kept in Heaven for us. We are protected by God's impregnable power in His domain where we are secure. And one day Jesus is coming for us in all His glory to take us to live with Him. Take a moment to send some praise His way. We are blessed!

# ⇒ WEEK 1 · DAY FOUR ⇐
## I PETER 1:6-9

Our study yesterday in 1 Peter 1:3-5 reminded us of some key theological concepts which the Apostle Peter shared with the believers in Asia Minor. As Christians, God the Father through His great mercy has bestowed upon us a new birth producing a living hope—salvation only possible because Jesus Christ conquered death through His resurrection. In addition, an imperishable, undefiled, unfading inheritance awaits us in Heaven protected by God's mighty power. In his letter, Peter urges the believers to greatly rejoice in all that God had provided for them. Take a moment, my friend, and do the same as we commence our study today.

As we begin, familiarize yourself with 1 Peter 1:6-9. Here Peter introduces his readers to the issue of trials which was an enduring thread throughout his letter. These believers were facing trials and Peter desires to reassure them and, in turn, others confronting the Christian's inevitable trials through the centuries.

1. Read John 15:18-21. What warning did Jesus give His disciples concerning their relationship to the world?

2. What points does Peter make about trials in verse 6?

Trials are a part of the human existence. While all of mankind face trials, Christians encounter the dimension of living in a fallen world amidst unbelievers. After all, we are not of this world, but merely sojourners passing through on our way to our eternal home. Peter knows that their trials are inescapable but temporary in light of eternity; in God's economy, trials are simply a segment of His refining process.

Warren Wiersbe gives some valuable insight into God's divine purpose in allowing the believer to suffer trials:

> When God permits His children to go through the furnace, He keeps His eye on the clock and His hand on the thermostat. If we rebel, He may have to reset the clock; but if we submit, He will not permit us to suffer one minute too long. The important thing is that we learn the lesson He wants to teach us and that we bring glory to Him alone. While we may not be able to rejoice as we look *around* in our trials, we can rejoice as we look *ahead*. [12]

3.  What do the following verses reveal about the refining process in a believer's life?

    Proverbs 17:3

    Isaiah 48:10

    Job 23:10

    Psalm 66:10

4.  List two results of testing through trials that Peter mentions in verse 7.

May Philippians 3:10 become our genuine desire and prayer: "...that I may know Him and the power of His resurrection and the fellowship of His sufferings, being conformed to His death." How unfathomable that because of our genuine faith, believers will share in Christ's praise, glory, and honor at His revelation. But first, we might experience "the fellowship of His sufferings."

5. According to James, the Lord's half-brother, in James 1:2-4, what does the testing of your faith develop within the believer?

6. Reflect back on a period in your life when you experienced testing through a trial. Did the Lord use it to refine you and to mature you spiritually? Record the details.

Peter had walked with Jesus throughout His earthly ministry. He had observed His miracles and listened to His teaching. He was present at the Transfiguration and in Gethsemane. He witnessed both the crucifixion and the resurrection of Christ. The original readers of Peter's letter had not seen Jesus during His ministry on earth, yet they loved Him and believed in Him.

7. As a result of living in faith, with what are believers filled? How would you define it? (vv. 8-9)

Though life could be hard, and persecution and trials would come, these Christians could greatly rejoice—with "joy inexpressible and full of glory."

Have you ever wondered how you would react when faced with a trial because of your faith? Christians throughout the centuries have dealt with such dilemmas. Early Christians bravely faced the lions, and countless missionaries have given their lives in a quest to share the gospel. Even as I write this study, an American missionary is imprisoned in Turkey. His name is Andrew Brunson, and his story has been in the news since he was arrested in 2016. Perhaps you have even lifted up his name in prayer in the last few months. He has lived in Turkey for over twenty years ministering to the Turkish people. His present saga began when he attempted to receive permanent citizenship. Instead, he was arrested and accused of being a part of a terrorist organization. Placed in an overcrowded cell, he has been persecuted, ridiculed for his faith, and physically broken. Meanwhile, his second trial has been postponed. According to those in contact with him, his greatest desire is to remain true to Christ. While in prison, he has written this song. Read it and pray for our brother in Christ.

**ANDREW'S SONG**

You are worthy, worthy of my all

My tears and pain I lift up as an offering

Teach me to share in the fellowship of your suffering

Lamb of God, you are worthy of my all

You are worthy, worthy of my all

Adopted as a son, a brother to my King

Indeed I will share in your glory if I share your suffering

Jesus, you are worthy of my all

You are worthy, worthy of my all

But my heart faints, drowned in sorrow, overwhelmed

Make me like you, cross-bearer, persevering, faithful to the end

To stand the trial and receive the crown of life

You are worthy, worthy of my all

This is my declaration in the darkest hour

Jesus, the Faithful One who loves me, always good and true

You made me yours, you are worthy of my all

I want to be found worthy to stand before you on that day

With no regrets from cowardice, things left undone

To hear you say, "Well done, my faithful friend, now enter your reward"

Jesus, my joy, you are the prize I'm running for

You are worthy, worthy of my all

You are worthy, worthy of my all

What can I give to the Son of God, who gave himself for me

Here I am, you are worthy of my all [13]


Jesus is worthy of our all!

As we concluded our study yesterday, we were reflecting on the salvation of our souls which generates inexpressible and glorious joy in the life of the believer. In the text, Peter reminds his readers that this great salvation, shaped within the heart of a holy God, had been prophesied by the prophets of old in their words and writings. The Old Testament prophets played a key role in God's revelation for He had not kept His salvation plan a secret, but had disclosed many of the details of the Messiah's suffering and glorification through the prophets. Let's take a few moments to consider the significance of the prophetic message in God's design to redeem mankind as we ponder our study passage for today.

According to the lexical aid in the *Hebrew-Greek Key Word Study Bible,* the Greek word *prophetes* "means one who speaks openly before anyone, and is the technical name for an interpreter of a divine message." [14] Additionally, this source says: "It is clear that what really characterized the prophet was immediate communion with God, a divine communication of what the prophet had to declare." [15] The lexical aid also reveals:

> Two things are necessary for a prophet: an insight granted by God into divine secrets or mysteries, and communicating these secrets to others. It includes God's concept of grace, but with the warnings, announcements of judgment, and so forth, pertaining thereto. In the case of the OT, prophetic preaching was foretelling of the salvation yet to be accomplished. In the NT, prophecy was a publication of the salvation already accomplished, so far at least as it did not concern itself with future realities. [16]

Read 1 Peter 1:10-11.

1.   What did the prophets puzzle about concerning the grace that was to come? (vv. 10-11)

2. What two things composed the general content of the prophetic message? (v. 11)

3. According to verse 11, who was the true Author of the Old Testament prophecies?

The inspiration of the Scripture is a very important concept to the Apostle Peter which he addresses in his second letter to the believers in Asia Minor. In 2 Peter 1:16-21, Peter provides an eyewitness account and a definitive word regarding prophecy

Read 2 Peter 2:16-21.

4. List the specific details Peter shares concerning his eyewitness experience with Jesus and his suggestion to his readers. (vv. 16-19)

5. What does Peter emphatically state concerning prophecy in verses 20-21?

We need only to open the Book of Acts to discover Peter's extensive knowledge of Messianic prophecy from the Old Testament. As the early church was born, he effectively weaves together prophecy and its subsequent fulfillment in Jesus Christ as he mightily preached the good news of the gospel, first to the Jews and then to the Gentiles.

6. Examine the accounts of Peter's sermons in these passages from Acts and make note of his effective use of prophecy to proclaim salvation through Jesus Christ. What was the result in each case?

Acts 2:14-41

Acts 3:12-4:4

Acts 10:34-45

Peter's passion for pointing out the fulfillment of Old Testament prophecy in Jesus Christ undoubtedly is drawn from his discipleship under Christ Himself. From the beginning of His public ministry until His post-resurrection appearances, Jesus presented Himself as the completion of prophetic predictions.

7. Read the following passages and relate what claims Jesus makes regarding Old Testament prophecies.

Luke 4:14-21

Luke 24:25-27

Luke 24:44-48

*The ESV Study Bible* substantiates our study:

When the Bible says that "he opened their minds to understand the *Scriptures*" (Luke 24:45), it cannot mean just a few scattered predictions about the Messiah. It means the OT as a whole, encompassing all three of the major divisions of the OT that the Jews traditionally recognized.

At the heart of understanding all these OT books is the truth that they point forward to the suffering of Christ, his resurrection, and the subsequent spread to the gospel to "all nations" (Luke 24:47). The OT as a whole, through its promises, its symbols, and its pictures of salvation, looks forward to the actual accomplishment of salvation that took place once for all in the life, death, and resurrection of Jesus Christ. [17]

The Messiah's suffering and future glory were revealed to the prophets by the Holy Spirit. They longed to know the how and the when, but it was shown to them that fulfillment lay in the future. Peter's first readers were the recipients of this great salvation through Christ's suffering and were awaiting His return, though for a little while they could anticipate various trials.

Thomas Schreiner reminds us: "Old Testament prophets saw it from afar, and angels also marvel when gazing upon what God has done in Christ, while the Petrine readers actually experience it." [18] And so, have we as believers. Rejoice, my friend!

# WEEK 2
## In Pursuit of Holiness
### 1 PETER 1:13-25

*But like the Holy One who called you, be holy yourselves also in all your behavior;*
*because it is written, "You shall be holy, for I am holy."*
1 Peter 1:15-16

*We're too Christian to enjoy sin and too sinful to enjoy Christ. We've got just enough*
*Jesus to be informed, but not enough to be transformed.[19]*
~ Mark Batterson, All In

It is in these verses in 1 Peter that we are given the secret to real happiness and joy. We all long for it. We secretly desire to live happily ever after and we sure would like it to start now! The issue with most of us is our unwillingness to fully surrender to Christ. Randy Alcorn recounts a conversation between Hannah Whitall Smith, the 19th century author of the classic on joyful Christianity, *The Christian's Secret of a Happy Life,* and her son Frank:

After coming to Christ, Hannah Whitall Smith warned her son Frank, "There is such a thing as having just enough religion to make one miserable, and as long as you hold back from a full surrender to His will, this will be the situation. Oh, do let Jesus have all of your heart! He will give you such a fullness of joy in Himself that will far more than repay you for any earthly pleasure you think you may miss because of it."[20]

Our greatest joy will be found in Jesus. Those are not just Sunday School words, they are truth. God has created us in His image and we were made for relationship. Sin has separated us from intimacy with God. It is sin and rebellion that destroy our happiness and ultimately lead to destruction. Through surrender, we experience the renewal of relationship with Christ and find our deepest needs met in Him. Then our joy will be as Peter described it: "you greatly rejoice with joy inexpressible and full of glory" (1 Peter 1:8).

As we learned in the Introduction, as we focus on the "small screen," God reveals the "big picture". His truth is revealed to those who have fully surrendered and thus are able to "see" spiritually the truths that God has revealed in Christ.

# WEEK 2 · DAY ONE

## 1 PETER 1:13-25

Fully surrendering to the Lord begins with your mind. As we move into our section of Scripture for this week, we are instructed to "prepare your minds for action." The best way to prepare your mind is to immerse it in Scripture. The Word of God is the Sword of the Spirit that we use against all errant thoughts.

Read 1 Peter 1:13-25.

The New King James Version of the Bible translates these opening words in verse 13 as, "Gird up the loins of your mind". Those are strange sounding words to our modern ears. But to Peter's intended audience they painted a vivid picture. In the New Testament era, people wore long flowing clothes. "The image is that of a robed man, tucking his skirts under the belt, so he can be free to run". [21] That visual makes me think about how the Israelites were instructed to eat the Passover before leaving Egypt. They were to eat it with their "loins girded and sandals on their feet" (Exodus 12:11, NASB). They were prepared for action.

1. Describe how you can "gird up your mind for action."




2 Corinthians 10:3-5 is the primary Scripture that I memorized to remind me to take my thoughts captive to the obedience of Christ. Read these verses.


2. What does this Scripture passage instruct us to do?

Read Romans 12:1-2.

Rarely does a day go by when I do not pray these verses for myself. If you have not memorized these verses, I would encourage you to write them out on a note card and begin to meditate on and memorize them.

3. How does Romans 12:2 tell us that we are transformed?

*Transformation into Christlikeness begins when the Word of God and the Spirit of God enter our hearts through our minds.*

Transformation into Christlikeness begins when the Word of God and the Spirit of God enter our hearts through our minds.

4. Look up the following verses and make notes on what they teach us about renewing our minds.

Romans 8:6

Philippians 2:5

Philippians 4:8

Colossians 3:2

5. Read the following verses, paying attention to the use of the word "sober": 1 Peter 4:7; 5:8; 2 Timothy 4:5; 1 Thessalonians 5:6-8; 1 Timothy 3:2. Based on these verses what does sober mean?

We must prepare our minds and be sober and ready for action. We have a race to run, a purpose to fulfill.

6. What has God revealed to you that is your "action" at this time in your life?

Read 1 Peter 1:13-25 again.

In verse 13, Peter tells us to "Fix your hope completely on the grace to be brought to you at the revelation of Jesus Christ."

1.  How do we "fix our hope"?

Regardless of what is going on around us, we must fix our minds beyond the present. Kenneth Wuest comments on verse 13, "Set your hope perfectly, unchangeably, without doubt and despondency."[22] This is not a passive action; it is an active choice we have to make over and over again.

As Christians, we long for the Second Coming of Christ and the Marriage Supper of the Lamb. When my three girls were planning their weddings, all of life moved into wedding mode. They dreamed about, talked about, and planned for that day. As believers, we are to live in expectation of "that day".

2.  How would living with this expectant hope change your life? (Take a few minutes to think about this and be specific in your answer.)

3.  Read Hebrews 12:1-2. On Whom are we to be fixed and what does this mean?

4.  Read Colossians 3:1-4. On what are we told to "set" our mind and how does this relate to fixing our hope?

Hope is defined as the "expectation of future good." [23] In the English language, we have lost much of this meaning of the word and tend to use "hope" as a synonym for "wish". For instance, perhaps we have an outdoor event scheduled for the weekend and we say "I hope it doesn't rain Saturday." "Hope" in that statement implies a certainty or confidence that it will not rain. The better word to use is "wish". "I wish that it would not rain on Saturday." However, Peter's use of the word "hope" in verse 13 is not a wish; it is certainty. He is telling them that without a doubt, that they can expect "future good."

5.  How can we personally fix our hope completely on the grace of Christ?

*When we accept moment to moment events and tribulations as the place where we*
*receive God's provision, we patiently anticipate the action of His Spirit in our lives.*
*In hope, we do our best to find and implement the ways in which our inner self*
*can take on the character of the children of the Highest.*
*This is the path of radical change...[24]*

~ Dallas Willard

Read 1 Peter 1:13-25 slowly. Reflect on each phrase.

In verse 14, Peter instructs us to be "obedient children". F.B. Meyer said, "It is impossible to exaggerate the importance of this truth. Obedience is not holiness; holiness is the possession of the soul by God. But holiness always leads to obedience." [25]

1.  How is obedience the outcome of holiness?

In his classic work, *The Pursuit of Holiness*, Jerry Bridges addresses the correlation of obedience to holiness:

> Too often, we say we are defeated by this or that sin. No, we are not defeated. We are simply disobedient. It might be good if we stop using the terms victory and defeat to describe our progress in holiness. Rather, we should use the terms obedience and disobedience. When I say I am defeated by some sin, I am unconsciously slipping out from under my responsibility. I am saying something outside of me has defeated me. But when I say I am disobedient, that places the responsibility for my sin squarely on me. We may in fact be defeated, but the reason we are defeated is because we have chosen to disobey.
>
> We need to brace ourselves up and to realize that we are responsible for thoughts, attitudes, and actions. We need to reckon on the fact that we died to sin's reign, that it no longer has any dominion over us, that God has united us with the risen Christ in all His power and has given us the Holy Spirit to work in us. Only as we accept our responsibility and appropriate God's provisions will we make any progress in our pursuit of holiness.[26]

The cry for holiness is a thread that runs throughout the Bible. God is the thrice holy God: "Holy, holy, holy is the Lord God, the Almighty" (Isaiah 6:3; Revelation 4:8). In verse 16, Peter is quoting Leviticus 11:44-45.

2. How are we to be holy as He is holy?

*Holiness* doesn't mean that we take a vow of abstinence from pleasure; it means that we acknowledge *Jesus* as the Source of life's greatest pleasure.

We know that our enemy is a liar and the father of lies (John 8:44). He wants to deceive us into thinking that to obey God is confining and takes away all the joy and happiness from our lives. When in reality, it is the sin that separates relationships and brings such great pain. The basic premise of Randy Alcorn's book, *Happiness,* is that holiness ultimately leads to our happiness. Alcorn quotes Jonathan Edwards who said, "Those that are highest in holiness [are] necessarily highest in happiness (for holiness and happiness are all one in heaven)". [27]

3. Write out your explanation of the connection between holiness and happiness.

Holiness doesn't mean that we take a vow of abstinence from pleasure; it means that we acknowledge Jesus as the Source of life's greatest pleasure. Alcorn also notes that Charles Spurgeon said, "Holiness is the royal road to happiness. The death of sin is the life of joy." [28]

4. How do we put sin to death?

Holy is defined as "moral and ethical wholeness or perfection; freedom from moral evil." [29]

5.   How can we, as marred image bearers, obey this command? (vv. 14-16)

For a little additional insight, consider the difference between the Old Covenant and the New Covenant. Hebrews 8 and 9 and 2 Corinthians 3 will prompt your memory on the differences.

6.   What have we received because of Christ?

*How little people know who think that holiness is dull. When one meets the real thing, it is irresistible. If even 10% of the world's population had it, would not the whole world be converted and happy before year's end?* [30]

~ C.S. Lewis

# ⇁ WEEK 2 • DAY FOUR ⇀
## 1 PETER 1:18-21

We are part of a redeemed race and should allow this truth to permeate our beings and transform our lives. Leviticus holds the key to understanding the death of Christ on the cross. One truth that stands out is the substitution of the innocent for the guilty. (Read Leviticus 1:4; 16:21-22.) That is why we should read God's Word in its entirety. All of the Old Testament points to what would one day be fulfilled in Christ.

Read 1 Peter 1:18-21.

We have not been purchased with corruptible things, but with the precious blood of the Lamb. Peter no doubt wanted to make the association with the lambs offered up day by day for the sins of the people.

1. From what does this passage tell us that Christ has redeemed us?

Christ's death was not an after thought, but determined in the mind of God before the creation of the world.

2. What does it mean that His death was "foreordained" (KJV) or "foreknown" (NASB) by God?

*God chose Him as your ransom long before the world began,*
*but He has now revealed him to you in these last days.*
1 Peter 1:20 (NLT)

The doctrine of the sacrifice of the innocent for the guilty began in Genesis. As Warren Wiersbe notes, "Isaac asked the question, 'Where is the lamb?' (Genesis 22:7) and John the Baptist answered it when he pointed to Jesus and said, 'Behold the Lamb of God which taketh away the sin of the world'" (John 1:29). [31] The blood is the life of all flesh. Life is God's gift to mankind and our supreme possession.

> Christianity is not just a set of rules to obey, but it is a *relationship* with Christ that should *change* what we *believe*, thus changing our actions.

3. Explain how Christ's blood purchases life for us.

Because Jesus gave His life for us, He demands that we come out and be separate for Him. The only way we can do this is through the power of His Spirit as we seek to obey His Word.

4. How are you appropriating your new life in Christ?

Dallas Willard writes, "The narrow gate is not, as so often assumed, doctrinal correctness. The narrow gate is obedience – and the confidence in Jesus necessary to it". [32]

5. What would you say causes you to doubt the Word of God and as a result to not obey Him fully?

Christianity is not just a set of rules to obey, but it is a relationship with Christ that should change what we believe, thus changing our actions.

*Nothing less than life in the steps of Christ is adequate to the human soul or the needs of our world. Any other offer fails to do justice to the drama of human redemption, deprives the hearer of life's greatest opportunity, and abandons this present life to the evil powers of the age. The correct perspective is to see following Christ not only as the necessity it is, but as the fulfillment of the highest human possibilities and as life on the highest plane.* [33]

~ Dallas Willard

It is only the Word of God that can purify our souls. That is exactly what Peter stated when he said, "you have purified your souls in obeying the truth through the Spirit" (1 Peter 1:22). It is through this purity that we are able to love one another with sincere love and do so fervently by the power of the Holy Spirit.

1.    What does it mean to "love one another fervently with a pure heart" (v. 22)?

Consider the Message translation of 1 Peter 1:22, "Now that you've cleaned up your lives by following the truth, love one another as if your lives depended on it."

2.    How do you best express love?

3.    Read Romans 12:10. How do you live out this verse?

4.    How would this kind of love impact your marriage, children or extended family?

5. Why is it sometimes harder to express fervent love to our family members?

Peter tells us that we have been born again, "not of corruptible seed but incorruptible" (v. 23). In his book, *The Divine Conspiracy,* Dallas Willard writes, "And what people do reveals, when thoroughly and honestly considered, the kind of person they really are (Matthew 7:16-20)." [34]

6. Since we act out of what we believe, how are your actions being impacted by your belief in God's Word?

7. The Bible clearly states that God's Word will stand forever (Isaiah 40:8; 1 Peter 1:24-25). How should this truth impact our lives?

Jesus said, "By this all men will know you are My disciples, if you have love for one another" (John 13:35). All of the Biblical writers express this same truth. 1 Corinthians 13 gives us a beautiful picture of the love that God provides and expects from His followers. Join me in praying that when others look at our lives, they will know we belong to Jesus by the way we love one another – in speech and action!

# WEEK 3

## As Living Stones

### 1 PETER 2:1-12

*And coming to Him as to a living stone which has been rejected by men, but is choice and precious in the sight of God, you also, as living stones, are being built up as a spiritual house for a holy priesthood, to offer up spiritual sacrifices acceptable to God through Jesus Christ.*

1 Peter 2:4-5

*We see the reality of Jesus risen, His actual existence now as a person who is present among His people. We find Him in His ecclesia, His sometimes motley but always glorious crew of called out ones.*[35]

~ Dallas Willard

Matthew Henry provides worthy commentary on I Peter 2:4-5:

The apostle here gives us a description of Jesus Christ as a living stone; and though to a capricious wit, or an infidel, this description may seem rough and harsh, yet to the Jews, who placed much of their religion in their magnificent temple, and who understood the prophetical style, which calls the Messiah a stone (Isaiah 8:14; 28:16), it would appear very elegant and proper. In this metaphorical description of Jesus Christ, He is called a stone, to denote His invincible strength and everlasting duration, and to teach his servants that He is their protection and security, the foundation on which they are built, and a rock of offence to all their enemies. He is the living stone, having eternal life in Himself, and being the prince of life to all His people. The reputation and respect He has with God and man are very different. He is disallowed of men, reprobated or rejected by his own countrymen the Jews, and by the generality of mankind; but chosen of God, separated and fore-ordained to be the foundation of the church, and precious, a most honourable, choice, worthy person in Himself, in the esteem of God, and in the judgment of all who believe on Him. To this person so described we are obliged to come: To whom coming, not by a local motion, for that is impossible since His exaltation, but by faith, whereby we are united to Him at first, and draw nigh to Him afterwards. Learn, Jesus Christ is the very foundation-stone of all our hopes and happiness.

He communicates the true knowledge of God (Matthew 11:27); by Him we have access to the Father (John 14:6), and through Him are made partakers of all spiritual blessings.[36]

Through Jesus Christ, we have been redeemed. We have been born again. We are living stones, having been indwelt by the Holy Spirit of God at the moment of conversion. We are being built up as a spiritual house to honor and serve God upon the precious Cornerstone, Jesus Christ. This is the source and the reason for our outrageous hope and extraordinary joy!

Peter begins this chapter by referring back to our great and glorious salvation. In 1 Peter 1:18-19, Peter writes, "For you were not redeemed with perishable things like silver or gold from your futile ways of life inherited from your forefathers, but with precious blood, as of a lamb unblemished and spotless, the blood of Christ." Peter continues the theme of our salvation, "You have been born again not of seed which is perishable but imperishable, that is, through the living and enduring Word of God" (1 Peter 1:23). Oh, the wonder of our salvation! "God demonstrated His own love toward us, in that while we were yet sinners, Christ died for us. Much more then, having now been justified by His blood, we shall be saved from the wrath of God through Him. For if while we were enemies we were reconciled to God through the death of His Son, much more, having been reconciled, we shall be saved by His life (Romans 5:8-10). In light of God's grace gift of salvation through Jesus Christ, our only reasonable response is to put "aside all malice and all deceit and hypocrisy and envy and all slander" (1 Peter 2:1) and aggressively pursue personal holiness and practical righteousness in daily living. In light of God's grace gift of salvation through Jesus Christ, our only reasonable reaction is outrageous hope and extraordinary joy!

"The living and enduring Word of God" (1 Peter 1:23b) was operational in our salvation and continues to be the source of our transformation through the process of sanctification.

# WEEK 3 · DAY ONE

## 1 PETER 2:1-3

Therefore, we are to put aside the old manner of living. Peter uses an imperative participle to instruct his readers to intentionally lay aside the sinful habit patterns of the old life. The verb Peter uses is translated "putting aside" and in the original language means "to put off or lay aside." His choice of words was sometimes used to indicate stripping off filthy garments. We are to put off the old filthy garments of the life prior to Christ and put on the new royal robes of righteousness provided by our new life in Christ.

Read 1 Peter 2:1-3.

1. We see this concept of putting aside the old manner of living in several places in Scripture. Look up the following references and write out what we are commanded to lay aside in order to live for the glory of God.

   Romans 13:12-14

   Ephesians 4:22-24

   Colossians 3:8-9

   Hebrews 12:1

   James 1:21

These verses are certainly not exhaustive, but give us a good working description of fleshly behavior we need to lay aside having come to the saving knowledge of Jesus Christ. After a genuine conversion, a changed life is enabled by the power of the Holy Spirit and therefore expected.

Peter connects the ability to lay aside sinful habit patterns of the old life to an unrelenting hunger for the Word of God. "Like newborn babies, long for the pure milk of the Word, so that by it you may grow in respect to salvation" (1 Peter 2:2). In the same way a newborn craves milk and refuses any other substitute, followers of Jesus should develop an insatiable appetite for the pure milk of the Word of God.

As women we readily understand Peter's illustration of a crying newborn. Many of us have walked the floor with a howling baby that refused to be quieted! We have all seen the red face, the clinched fists, the pinched forehead, and the wrinkled brow of a tiny infant that is intent on being fed and extremely annoyed by the delay of the forthcoming milk. A newborn will not be distracted and will not be denied. It is milk, or else! That is the way we should feel about the Word of God. We should crave it like a newborn that instinctively knows that milk is the only sustenance between life and starving to death.

2a. Look up Psalm 42:1-2. How does the psalmist describe his desire to know God?

2b. How would you describe your heart's desire towards the things of God?

2c. With God's help, what areas of your spiritual life do you desire to improve?

We live in the country, and nearly every morning five or six deer come to our pond to drink and graze in the cool grass tinged with the morning dew. It is a beautiful pastoral scene. I always think of this passage when I see them, and I ask myself, "Do I hunger and thirst after God?" Beloved daughter of the King, Peter strongly admonishes us to long for "the pure milk of the Word, so that by it you may grow in respect to salvation."

The continual pursuit of God's Word, mixed with our obedience to it, will result in healthy spiritual growth. This is not only a New Testament principle. This truth is reiterated many times in the Old Testament.

3. Look up Psalm 19:7-11. How does David describe God's Word?

The desire and need for food as physical sustenance is often used in the Bible to describe our spiritual relationship with the Word of God. In Psalm 81:10, God says, "Open your mouth wide and I will fill it." Further down in the chapter, God says, "I would feed you with the finest of the wheat; and with honey from the rock I would satisfy you" (Psalm 81:16). God wants to feed us from His Word. All He asks of us is to develop an appetite for the things of God.

We have a bluebird box on our property and every spring we discover four beautiful turquoise eggs tucked safely in the pine needle nest. The box has a hinged top, and every day I make a trek out to check on the progress of the baby birds.

Oddly, bluebirds are not threatened by human contact and actually seem to be happy to share the miracle of their expanding family with their human counterparts. The mother usually sits on a branch overhead and patiently watches as I open the top of the bluebird house and look in on her brood. Maybe she recognizes that I am also a mother and would never harm one of her offspring. At any rate, I love to watch this marvel of God's design in the animal kingdom.

Once hatched, the little bald fledglings shriek wildly when I carefully lift the lid and peek inside their wooden incubator. With wobbly necks outstretched, four little yellow beaks open wide as they beg for a morsel of food. That is the picture the psalmist is painting for us. God says to us, "Open your mouth wide and I will fill it." Just "as the deer pants for the water brooks, I desire for you to seek after My Word and My wisdom."

Sadly, we are in the habit of filling up on junk food and rejecting God's choice wheat and honey. Proverbs 27:7 says, "A sated man loathes honey, but to a famished man any bitter thing is sweet." Often, we become satiated on the temporal things the world has to offer and have no appetite for God's Word.

The boys and their wives treated us to an all-you-can-eat buffet for Father's Day. The tables groaned under the artistically arrayed trays of food. This feast for the eyes was not only lovely to look at, it was also unbelievably good, and we ate our fill. Even though a huge banquet spread still beckoned us, we were all suddenly so full that nothing looked appetizing. We could not be tempted to eat another bite even though the food was scrumptious and plentiful. In the same way, we need to beware of filling up on anything other than "the pure milk of the Word, so that you may grow in respect to salvation" (I Peter 2:2).

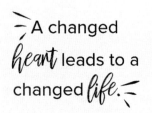
A changed *heart* leads to a changed *life.*

Peter's letter places a great significance on the believer's behavior. "If you have tasted the kindness of the Lord" (1 Peter 2:3) and have experienced genuine conversion, then pursue a working understanding of the Word of God in order to grow into spiritual maturity. A changed heart leads to a changed life. Malice, guile, hypocrisy, envy, and slander are just a few of the characteristics Peter mentions that have no place in the private or public persona of a child of God. The way to rid one's life of such deviant behavior is through the practice of the Word of God and the power of the Holy Spirit of God.

In the Sermon on the Mount Jesus says, "Blessed are those who hunger and thirst for righteousness, for they shall be satisfied" (Matthew 5:6). A lack of hunger for the things of God may well be an indication of a lack of genuine conversion. On the contrary, a genuine unquenchable hunger for the things of the Lord strongly indicates a genuine conversion experience. "Like newborn babies, long for the pure milk of the Word, so that by it you may grow in respect to salvation" (1 Peter 2:2). This is the pathway for experiencing the outrageous hope and extraordinary joy of Jesus!

In 1993, the Lord led my husband and I to relocate our family from the heart of the suburbs of Cordova to rural Fayette County. As young marrieds, we had bought ten acres of Fayette soybean fields in 1976 to plant as a tree farm to support our landscaping business. Little did we dream that one day we would build our home on this property and move the family to the country. As a city girl, born and bred, I must admit that certain aspects of country living were daunting to me at first, but I soon gave in to the gentle seductions of rural living. The star-studded black night sky without the intrusion of street lights, the symphonic serenade of crickets, the sweet scent of fresh turned earth, the mournful howl of coyotes, and the absence of invasive city sounds caused me to quickly embrace the pleasantries of country living.

The process of building a house was new to me, and I vacillated between ecstasy and insanity! Perhaps you cannot relate if you have never built a home, but the maddening process of dealing with multiple contractors who promise you deadlines, and then deliver disappointment caused me no small measure of aggravation. However, I did enjoy watching the building process as a plot of land was cleared, the foundation was laid, and a house slowly emerged from the rubble, brick upon brick.

In 1 Peter 2:4-5, Peter paints yet another picture for us, this one relating to the building of the church with living stones. Peter references Christ as "a living stone" on whom we, "as living stones are being built up as a spiritual house" for the glory of God.

Read 1 Peter 2:4-5.

In the Old Testament, Moses refers to God as The Rock. Deuteronomy 32:3-4 says, "For I proclaim the name of the Lord; ascribe greatness to our God! The Rock! His work is perfect, for all His ways are just; a God of faithfulness and without injustice, righteous and upright is He." This is significant since most of the believers in the early church were Jewish Christians, to whom the Old Testament was precious and quite familiar. In the New Testament, Jesus Christ is referred to as the Rock, the Stone on which the church rests. 1 Corinthians 10:4 says, "All [speaking of the children of Israel in the wilderness] drank the same spiritual drink, for they were drinking from the spiritual rock which followed them; and the rock was Christ."

Jesus Christ is the solid Rock of our salvation. In the Gospel of Luke, the Lord uses an analogy to illustrate this point.

Read Luke 6:46-49 and answer the following questions.

1a.  To whom does the Lord liken the one who "comes to me and hears My words and acts on them"?

1b.  When dire circumstances occur, what happens to the house built on the rock?

1c.  In contrast, what happens to the house built on sand when the storms of life batter it?

1d.  What is the conclusion of the analogy and what can we learn from it?

We come to Jesus for **salvation**, which results in the progressive transformation known as **sanctification**, whereby we are gradually made more like Jesus. This process is aided through regular exposure to strong Bible preaching and teaching, fellowship with the community of Christ, personal Bible study, commitment to regular prayer time, meditation on the Word, and memorization of Scripture, just to name a few. In addition, a genuine heart of obedience to God's revelation is imperative to precipitate a changed life. Here Peter speaks of coming to Jesus as "a living stone." His phraseology in the original language encompasses more than an initial conversion experience. It has the idea of drawing near to the Lord Jesus in intimate, personal ongoing communion. Song of Solomon 6:3 says, "I am my beloved's and my beloved is mine."

Jesus Christ "has been rejected by men, but is choice and precious in the sight of God." John 1:11 says, "He came to His own, and those who were His own did not receive Him." The Jews by and large rejected Jesus as the Messiah, but Peter has the larger wholesale rejection of the Lord Jesus by sinful humanity in mind.

Read John 3:19-20.

2.  Why did humanity reject Jesus?

The rejection of Jesus was prophesied long before His earthly incarnation as the Babe of Bethlehem. Isaiah 53:3 says "He was despised and forsaken of men, a man of sorrows and acquainted with grief; and like one from whom men hide their face He was despised, and we did not esteem Him." Jesus "has been rejected by men, but is choice and precious in the sight of God" (1 Peter 2:4). Paul writes, "God highly exalted Him, and bestowed on Him the name which is above every name" (Philippians 2:9).

In spite of those who have rejected Jesus, many have come to Him in repentance and faith and been gloriously saved. At the moment of conversion, the Lord places believers into the body of Christ and the family of God as "living stones" (I Peter 2:5).

3.  Read Ephesians 2:19-22. How does Paul describe us prior to conversion and then after salvation?

The true church is a holy habitation for the Lord constructed of individual believers who are being fashioned and hand-hewn into building blocks. The grout which cements us together is the Holy Spirit of God. As God chisels away our individual defects and flaws, sands off our rough edges, and smooths out our imperfections; we are able to be more perfectly fitted into the church of the Lord Jesus Christ.

Beloved, we are "living stones", but we are also "a holy priesthood" tasked with offering up "spiritual sacrifices acceptable to God through Jesus Christ" (1 Peter 2:5). Under the new covenant, we serve as priests, not in a building or a temple, but through sacrificial service expressed through our bodies. Each believer is the "temple of the Holy Spirit who is in you, whom you have from God" (1 Corinthians 6:19). Paul captures this same idea when he writes, "Therefore I urge you, brethren, by the mercies of God, to present your bodies a living and holy sacrifice, acceptable to God, which is your spiritual service of worship" (Romans 12:1). The only reasonable response to so great a salvation is a life surrendered to Jesus Christ and marked with works of righteousness on His behalf as living stones. The by-product of such a life built on the outrageous hope of the Lord is His extraordinary joy!

In today's passage, Peter quotes Old Testament passages (Isaiah 28:16, Psalm 118:22, and Isaiah 8:14), with which his original Jewish readers would have been very familiar, as he constructs his analogy of Christ as our Cornerstone.

Read I Peter 2:6-8.

This is not the first time Peter has referred to Jesus as the Chief Cornerstone. In Acts 4:11 when Peter addresses the Jewish rulers, elders, and scribes in Jerusalem he says, "He (referring to Jesus) is the stone which was rejected by you, the builders, but which became the Chief Cornerstone" (parenthesis mine).

As we delve into this passage, please keep in mind that Jesus applied the imagery of the Chief Cornerstone in Psalm 118:22 to Himself. "Jesus said to them, 'Did you never read in the Scriptures, The stone which the builders rejected, this became the Chief Cornerstone; this came about from the Lord, and it is marvelous in our eyes'?" (Matthew 21:42).

Sometimes a cornerstone may mean the keystone that is placed in the center of an arch, but in this context, it seems to refer to the foundation stone. In architecture the cornerstone established the configuration and construction of the building. Peter is using this visual to illustrate the centrality of Jesus Christ in the life of individual believers as well as the church at large. Jesus is the "choice Stone, a precious Cornerstone, and he who believes in Him will not be disappointed" (1 Peter 2:6).

I cannot help but think Peter's discourse on Christ our Cornerstone was prompted by a recollection from his time with Jesus in His earthly Incarnation that was pressed deeply into his memory bank.

Read Matthew 16:13-18.

1a. In this passage, Jesus asks His disciples who the people were saying that He was. What answers did the disciples give Him?

The supernatural works of Jesus could not be denied by the Jews, but most refused to acknowledge Him as Messiah. Jesus' question to His twelve disciples then becomes more pointed.

1b.  What does Jesus ask?

1c.  How does Peter respond?

Jesus replies to Peter using his family name, Simon Barjona. Peter's relationship to his earthly father is of no value for the sin issue in Peter's heart. Only a right relationship with God the Father through Jesus Christ matters!

1d.  What does Jesus say to Peter concerning God's divine revelation to him?

The reality of Jesus' divinity and Messiahship has already been established in the heart and mind of Peter and, since he often was the spokesman for the twelve, they, too, had come to fully believe (with the exception of Judas). The disciples had a front row seat to Jesus' earthly ministry. They witnessed His preaching and teaching, the miracles, the healings, and even His power over death and the grave.

But it was not their experiences with the Lord that brought them to the point of belief. Flesh and blood cannot reveal the truth of God's provision of Christ's sacrificial atonement. Only the Father could convict them of their sin and convince them of their need of a Savior. Only God can draw sinners to repentance and salvation through Jesus.

In Matthew 16:18, Jesus speaks truth into Peter's life, "I also say to you that you are Peter, and upon this rock I will build My church". Many commentators believe Jesus is using a play on words to make His point. The name Peter is a Greek word for a small stone or pebble. The word He uses for rock means a rocky mountain or peak. Jesus is comparing Peter, a small stone, to the giant boulder on which He would build His church. Similarly, in his epistle Peter refers to individual believers as "living stones" being built upon the "choice Stone, [the] precious Cornerstone," which is the Lord Jesus Christ.

Perhaps from personal experience Peter adds, "He who believes in Him will not be disappointed" (1 Peter 2:6). Despite the present suffering many of Peter's readers were experiencing, the surpassing greatness of knowing Jesus Christ as Lord and Savior would cause them to "greatly rejoice with joy inexpressible and full of glory" (1 Peter 1:8). Jesus does not disappoint, and a life lived for Him is not only worthwhile now, it results in eternal reward. Jesus said, "Do not store up for yourselves treasures on earth, where moth and rust destroy, and where thieves break in and steal. But store up for yourselves treasures in heaven, where neither moth nor rust destroy, and where thieves do not break in or steal; for where your treasure is, there your heart will be also" (Matthew 6:19-21).

Despite God's gracious offer of salvation through Jesus Christ, many reject Him. For those who "are disobedient to the Word, Jesus becomes a stone of stumbling and a rock of offense" (1 Peter 2:8). The cross of Jesus Christ is an offense to the unsaved heart and mind. It convicts and condemns the unrepentant sinner to eternal damnation. Romans 1:18-20 says, "For the wrath of God is revealed from heaven against all ungodliness and unrighteousness of men who suppress the truth in unrighteousness, because that which is known about God is evident within them; for God made it evident to them. For since the creation of the world His invisible attributes, His eternal power and divine nature, have been clearly seen, being understood through what has been made, so that they are without excuse."

God has created a God-shaped void in the heart of every human being. He has revealed Himself through the divine genius of His creation. Even the heavens declare the glory of God. Psalm 19:1 says, "The heavens are telling of the glory of God; and their expanse is declaring the work of His hands." Psalm 97:6 says, "The heavens declare His righteousness, and all the peoples have seen His glory." Psalm 98:2 says, "The Lord has made known His salvation; He has revealed His righteousness in the sight of the nations." He has made Himself known through His creation, His Son, and by His Word. In Romans 2:1a, Paul explains, "Therefore you are without excuse."

With undeniable clarity, God has made Himself known. Hebrews 1:1-3 says, "God, after He spoke long ago to the fathers in the prophets in many portions and in many ways, in these last days has spoken to us in His Son, whom He appointed heir of all things, through whom also He made the world. And He is the radiance of His glory and the exact representation of His nature." The soul that rejects grace and scorns salvation is eternally damned to hell because he/she has willfully refused Jesus Christ and trampled His blood underfoot. There always has been and always will be those who reject the Lord of glory.

In I Corinthians 1:18, Paul notes, "For the word of the cross is foolishness to those who are perishing." Paul goes on to write that the cross of Christ was a stumbling block to the religious Jews and foolishness to the intellect of the pagan Gentiles. In I Corinthians 2:14, Paul explains, "A natural man does not accept the things of the Spirit of God, for they are foolishness to him; and he cannot understand them, because they are spiritually appraised." The cross was, and still is, the offense. In order to be saved, one must first recognize the sinful condition of his or her heart, repent, believe on the Lord Jesus' once-for-all sacrifice for sin, and receive Him by faith. To those who come to Him for salvation He is "a choice stone, a precious cornerstone." This is the outrageous hope that produces the extraordinary joy of Jesus in us!!

# ⇥ WEEK 3 · DAY FOUR ⇤
## I PETER 2:9-10

In our study today, we will catch just a glimpse of the spiritual blessings we possess through our personal relationship with Jesus. This is in stark contrast with those who reject Him, who "stumble because they are disobedient to the word" (I Peter 2:8). Eternal destruction will be the result of those who refuse the grace gift of salvation.

We who have received Jesus Christ through repentance and faith (see Acts 20:20-21) have been placed into the family of God and the body of Christ. In light of so great a salvation Paul writes, "I count all things to be loss in view of the surpassing value of knowing Christ Jesus my Lord, for whom I have suffered the loss of all things, and count them but rubbish so that I may gain Christ, and may be found in Him, not having a righteousness of my own derived from the Law, but that which is through faith in Christ, the righteousness which comes from God on the basis of faith, that I may know Him and the power of His resurrection and the fellowship of His sufferings, being conformed to His death; in order that I may attain to the resurrection of the dead" (Philippians 3:8-11). Oh, the glories of our salvation! The outrageous hope and extraordinary joy we have in Jesus!

We are currently living in what is known as "the church age." The church age was ushered in 50 days after the Passover meal was commemorated on the eve of the crucifixion of Christ. A gathering of about one hundred twenty Jesus followers huddled in the Upper Room on the Day of Pentecost. The Holy Spirit descended to indwell each individual follower of Jesus (see Acts 2:1-4). Peter, writing to primarily Jewish Christian readers, shows how the Old Testament ideas of the temple, the priests, and the sacrificial system all have new meanings in Jesus.

Read I Peter 2:9-10.

Peter depicts the church using imageries similar to those used of Israel in the Old Testament. However, this in no way implies that the church deposes Israel or is the recipients of the national blessings promised to the Jewish people. Just as Israel was central to God's redemptive plan in the Old Testament, so the church is central to God's sovereign purposes in the New Testament.

After the death, burial, and resurrection of Jesus Christ, God began building "a spiritual house for a holy priesthood, to offer up spiritual sacrifices acceptable to God through Jesus Christ" (1 Peter 2:5). Christ is the Cornerstone; His followers are the "living

> *Considering what God has done on our behalf, the only reasonable response is the aggressive pursuit of personal holiness and practical righteousness.*

stones" being built upon Him. God is building His church, a new "chosen race." This time His people will not descend from a particular family or race, but from those who have a personal relationship with Him through Jesus Christ, His Son.

Beloved, our privileged position in Jesus Christ carries with it great responsibility. We are to "proclaim the excellencies of Him who has called [us] out of darkness into His marvelous light" (1 Peter 2:9). Understanding who we are in Christ is foundational for our ability to fulfill this mandate.

In Scripture, conversion is often depicted as a transfer from darkness to light.

Read Paul's prayer recorded in Colossians 1:9-14.

1a. Paul lists his desires for all believers. What are they?

1b. What has God done for us through Jesus Christ?

Considering what God has done on our behalf, the only reasonable response is the aggressive pursuit of personal holiness and practical righteousness.

2a. Read John 8:12. What title does Jesus assign to Himself?

2b.  What qualities will (should) characterize His children?

A changed heart should be revealed through a transformed life. While this change is progressive, evidence of a genuine conversion should be readily seen in those of us claiming to know Jesus.

In Ephesians 4:1-3, Paul urges followers of Jesus to pursue holy living.

3.  What does he urge us to do?

Paul continues the theme of holy living throughout most of his writings.

4.  Read Ephesians 5:8-10. Considering our former state prior to our conversion, how should we now live?

We are called to walk in the Light as children of Light. John writes, "God is Light, and in Him there is no darkness at all. If we say that we have fellowship with Him and yet walk in the darkness, we lie and do not practice the truth; but if we walk in the Light as He Himself is the Light, we have fellowship with one another, and the blood of Jesus His Son cleanses us from all sin" (1 John 1:5-7). Our right standing in the Kingdom of God provides community with brothers and sisters in Christ. When we walk in the Light we enjoy fellowship and community with one another and "indeed our fellowship is with the Father, and His Son Jesus Christ" (1 John 1:3).

God "called [us] out of darkness into His marvelous light; for [we] once were not a people, but now [we] are the people of God; [we] had not received mercy, but now [we] have received mercy" (1 Peter 2:9-10). We are sinners by birth, by nature, and by choice. Romans 3:23 says, "For all have sinned and fall short of the glory of God." Sin separated us from God. "The wages of sin is death, but the free gift of God is eternal life in Christ Jesus our Lord" (Romans 6:23). Christ died for our sins and paid our debt in full with His blood. He offers us the free gift of eternal life which we receive by repentance and faith. Repent. Believe. Receive Christ and be saved. "Whoever will call on the name of the Lord will be saved" (Romans 10:13). In Jesus Christ, we have received mercy. Christ became sin for us and took the wrath of God which we deserved. Therefore, it is left to us to "proclaim the excellencies" of the outrageous hope and extraordinary joy of Jesus in us!!

# WEEK 3 · DAY FIVE
## 1 PETER 2:11-12

Much of Peter's letter has to do with our behavior, our public persona. He is concerned that our manner of life validates our testimony rather than contradict it. Peter had the experience of Pentecost behind him and he is drawing on personal experience. He knows the powerful persuasion of the reality of Christ demonstrated by the power of the Holy Spirit. Peter has firsthand knowledge of the winsome nature of a life yielded to God. He is well aware of the need for holy living. He urges believers to live lives of personal holiness and practical righteousness.

Read I Peter 2:11-12.

We are beloved of God. As John writes, "See how great a love the Father has bestowed on us, that we should be called children of God; and such we are" (1 John 3:1). We are the happy recipients of God's unfathomable love and we belong to Him. "Our citizenship is in Heaven, from which also we eagerly wait for a Savior, the Lord Jesus Christ" (Philippians 3:20). Therefore, we are merely "aliens and strangers" passing through this world on the way home (I Peter 2:11).

1.  Read Hebrews 13:14. How does this verse characterize our alien-status as Christians?

We are "looking for the city which has foundations, whose architect and builder is God" (Hebrews 11:10). While we live **in this world**, we are no longer **of this world**. Consequently, we are implored to "abstain from freshly lusts which wage war against the soul" (1 Peter 2:11).

2a.  Read Galatians 5:16-17. Describe the raging internal conflict.

2b. How can we abstain from fleshly behavior?

*Even though regeneration produces a new disposition with holy longings, that new life force remains incarcerated within the old, unredeemed human flesh, precipitating an ongoing battle between the spirit and the flesh. Nevertheless, believers are no longer slaves of unrighteousness, and sin is not their master—they are free from its dominant and exclusive power.*[37]
~ John MacArthur

The Spirit of God enables us to resist the downward pull of the world, the flesh, and the devil. Therefore, Peter challenges us, "Keep your behavior excellent among the Gentiles, so that in the thing in which they slander you as evildoers, they may because of your good deeds, as they observe them, glorify God in the day of visitation" (1 Peter 2:12). Sadly, it is often the behavior of the church, the body of Christ, which gives offense and causes unbelievers to question the validity of our message. We must be careful not to become a stumbling block to another believer (or an unbeliever for that matter) by our behavior or manner of speech. In Romans 14:13, Paul cautions, "Determine this—not to put an obstacle or a stumbling block in a brother's way." We are called to holy living. The cross of Christ is to be the offense, not the Christian. Colossians 3:17 says, "Whatever you do in word or deed, do all in the name of the Lord Jesus, giving thanks through Him to God the Father."

The apostle Paul voices a similar concern, knowing that the lifestyle of individual believers preaches a powerful message for or against the power of Christ. Paul is determined on "giving no cause for offense in anything, in order that the ministry be not discredited" (2 Corinthians 6:3). The most powerful gospel message preached is not from the pulpit but from the lifestyle of every child of God.

3. Read 2 Corinthians 5:17-20. In this passage Paul lays down some powerful truths for pure living. What insight can you glean about the calling of personal holiness that is on our lives?

As to our standing, we are seated with Christ in the heavenlies. As to our state, we are aliens and strangers marching on to glory. We are citizens of Heaven through faith in Jesus Christ, therefore, our behavior should be excellent.

Keeping oneself untainted from the toxic contaminates of this world should be a full-time pursuit of every child of God. The ability to do so is traced back to a working knowledge of the Word of God. To the degree you are able to rightly divide God's Word and obey it is the degree you will be victorious in your Christian life. In the High Priestly Prayer Jesus prays, "I do not ask Thee to take them out of the world, but to keep them from the evil one. They are not of the world, even as I am not of the world. Sanctify them in the truth; Thy word is truth" (John 17:15-17). The key to remaining unblemished and unstained by the foul pollutants of this world is to saturate your soul with the Word of God, surrender your will in obedience to it, and yield yourself to the power of the indwelling Holy Spirit.

> The key to remaining unblemished and unstained by the foul pollutants of this world is to *saturate* your soul with the Word of God, *surrender* your will in obedience to it, and *yield* yourself to the power of the indwelling Holy Spirit.

In Colossians 3:5-17, Paul gives us a thumbnail sketch of a life surrendered to the Lord and saturated with the Word.

4a. Read this passage and make a list of the characteristics of the flesh and the qualities of the Spirit-filled life. Circle the traits that typify your lifestyle.

| THE FLESH-DOMINATED LIFE | THE SPIRIT-FILLED LIFE |
| --- | --- |
|  |  |

4b.  What issues do you need to work on?

4c.  What plan of action do you need to enable change?

Beloved, the Christian life is not meant to be a passive experience, but rather an aggressive pursuit of the things of God. When we live intentionally, engaged in keeping our behavior excellent before the lost world, others will see the outrageous hope and extraordinary joy of Jesus Christ in us.

# WEEK 4
## For All To See

### 1 PETER 2:13-25

*For you have been called for this purpose, since Christ also suffered for you,*
*leaving you an example for you to follow in His steps.*
1 Peter 2:21

The fact that I'm a woman doesn't make me a different kind of Christian, but the fact
that I'm a Christian does make me a different kind of woman. [38]
~ Elisabeth Elliott

Jesus Christ. The perfect, sinless Son of God. He is our example. He is our Standard. No other comparison will do. Let us passionately pursue the Scripture this week in order to understand our calling as a Christ follower. May it be done for the Lord's sake...for all to see! And when we go after Him in this way, with a pure heart, we will experience extravagant joy.

## WEEK 4 · DAY ONE

I think that most of us would agree that submission to authority is one of the most difficult doctrines to obey. We struggle with giving up the right to make decisions for ourselves. And we really don't like the idea of someone else telling us what to do. To be honest, rules and regulations that restrict us just rub us the wrong way. Paraphrasing Isaiah 53:6, we've all gone our own way, and by nature we are rebels at heart.

Read 1 Peter 2:13-14.

1.  What should be our reason for submitting to human authority?

We could stop right here and spend significant time on this phrase. <u>For the Lord's sake.</u> This should be our sole purpose for obeying or submitting to any command in Scripture. Why should our children obey us? Why should we, as wives, submit to our husbands? Why should we minister to the poor and hurting? Why should we bear one another's burdens? All of these things should be done for the sake of the name of Jesus Christ (3 John 1:7).

Read Colossians 3:17.

2.  What instruction does Peter give in this verse?

Merriam-Webster defines *whatever* as "anything or everything, no matter what, any and all."[39] I would say the Scripture is clear. Anything and everything I do should be for His sake, bringing glory and honor to His name. Peter is giving us this same instruction in the area of submitting to and respecting human authority. Most of us would agree that this is a fleeting practice in today's society. We see evidence of this in our homes, schools, churches and communities.

The Life Application Study Bible notes, "When Peter told his readers to respect all human authority, he was speaking of the Roman Empire under Nero, a notoriously cruel tyrant. Obviously he was not telling believers to compromise their consciences; as Peter had told the high priest years earlier, 'We must obey God rather than any human authority' (Acts 5:29). But in most aspects of daily life, it was possible and desirable for Christians to live according to the law of their land."[40]

3. What are some ways you can submit to and respect human authority? When do you find it most difficult to do so?

Read Romans 13:1-5 and answer the following questions.

4a. From where does authority come? (v. 1)

4b. When we rebel, against whom are we rebelling? What is the result? (v. 2)

4c. Why are authorities given to us? (v. 4)

4d. What is the result of submitting to human authority? (v. 5)

As we have read, the Bible is clear on how we are to believe and behave in this area. We have a mandate as well as personal responsibility in how we respond to human authority. Choosing anything less is disobedience and rebellion to God Almighty.

Whether it be politics, religion, or some other hot button topic, we are bombarded daily with a wide array of thoughts and opinions. As we consider holiness (1 Peter 1) and shining like stars in a dark world (Philippians 2), may we be challenged and committed to surrendering this area of our lives to the complete control of the Holy Spirit. Our flesh does not like to be told what to do. If you doubt this, go spend some time in any nursery or preschool. (You could even come to my house and observe me from time to time.) From the beginning, mankind has rebelled against God and fought the urge to have his or her own way.

This lost and dying world, which grows increasingly dark, must see followers of Christ standing out, radically different than the norm. Respecting and submitting to authority that God has put into place is a sure way to be set apart...especially when we disagree.

Referencing the text from Romans 13, Pastor Steven J. Cole concludes the following:

> Our text rests on the assumption that you are in subjection to God and want to please Him. Paul is not promoting moralism, but rather submission to the lordship of Jesus Christ. He is showing us how that submission plays out in our relationship to our government. So before you get right with the government, you've got to get right with God by repenting of your sins and trusting in Jesus Christ as Savior and Lord. Your relationship with Christ provides the basis for proper submission toward the government.[41]

As we conclude today, I encourage you to do a couple of things.

First, take a moment to go before the Lord and honestly evaluate your heart. Where does your mind immediately go when you think of a human authority with whom you disagree (employer, pastor, President, other government leaders, teacher, etc.)? Do you need to confess and repent of a bad attitude or a rebellious spirit? Commit afresh and anew to surrender this area to the lordship of Jesus Christ.

Secondly, I urge you to pray for the authorities in your life. The most effective way to reach and minister to the hearts of those in authority is to faithfully pray for them. 1 Timothy 2:2 tells us, "Pray this way for kings and and all who are in authority so that we can live peaceful and quiet lives marked by godliness and dignity" (NLT). When we pray, we are the beneficiaries.

5. What are some specific scriptures to pray for those in authority?

*Christian freedom does not mean being free to do as we like;*

*it means being free to do as we ought.* [42]

~ William Barclay

Have you ever been mocked or ridiculed for your beliefs? Have you been falsely accused of something? In today's text, Peter tells us one of the reasons for submission is to silence foolish accusations that come against us.

Read I Peter 2:15-16.

Rather than responding in anger or seeking revenge, we are called to respond according to God's Word, submitting to His ways rather than our own. Proverbs 3:5 tells us to "Trust in the LORD with all your heart; do not depend on your own understanding" (NLT).

Life can be unfair at times, especially when we feel attacked. It can be burdensome and weary. Perhaps, you find yourself feeling hopeless at times. God not only wants us to experience hope, but His desire is that we know outrageous hope. Romans 15:13 tells us that by the power of the Holy Spirit, we can abound in and overflow with hope.

We see from Scripture that God's will is that we live honorable lives, even in the face of injustice. This silences those who speak out against us. Again, this is a contrary belief system to our society's way of thinking. The world says, "You don't deserve that" or "I'll make sure she gets what's coming to her!"

Last week's study reminded us that, "...you are a chosen people. You are royal priests, a holy nation, God's very own possession. As a result, you can show others the goodness of God..." (1 Peter 2:9, NLT). We have been chosen by God as His very own. We are called to represent Him, and by doing so, we show His goodness to others. What a powerful position and incredible privilege!

1.   Read the following verses. How do these truths speak to you as you consider honorable living?


     Proverbs 21:21



     1 Timothy 4:12 (Consider as counsel for your children, grandchildren, or a new believer.)



     2 Timothy 2:2

Titus 2:3-5 (Specifically as a woman)



1 Peter 2:11




Challenge yourself. How do you conduct yourself among non-believers? Are you a faithful witness for God to your family members, neighbors, and coworkers? Do you behave dishonorably before the world? Spend some time in prayer today, asking God to help you be obedient to the call to live honorably in this pagan world. When tempted to act dishonorably, remember that you are a witness for Christ at all times. You have been given power to silence ignorance and to reflect God's goodness by living honorably.

Today's text goes on to say that we are free! If you've spent any time in church, "freedom in Christ" is a phrase with which you are well acquainted. If you have made a decision to repent from your sin and accept Jesus Christ, by faith, as your Savior, you are free! (If you've not yet made this decision, please refer to the appendix in the back of this book entitled "How To Become A Christian." This is the most important decision of your life.)

As children of God, we are truly free. We are free from hell and eternal separation from God. We are free from sin. It has no power over us, except that which we give it. True to His nature and character, God has also given us freedom to choose. While He desires that all men be saved (1 Timothy 2:3-4), God does not force us to choose salvation in Jesus Christ.


2. Look back at 1 Peter 2:16a. How can we, as Christ followers, be free AND be slaves? (Use Scripture to support your answer.)








As believers, we get to choose our Master!

It is true! We are free to choose, however, Scripture clearly commands that we not use our freedom as an excuse to do evil. There are two choices: slaves of sin or slaves of obedience.

J. Vernon McGee speaks to liberty in this way:

> The relationship of the believer to other people is a testimony which speaks louder than the message from the pulpit. You see, the believer in Christ has a liberty which the man outside of Christ does not have. Believers have a marvelous liberty in Christ Jesus. I personally believe that I could go places and see things which the average Christian could not. Although I don't think I would be hurt by them, I avoid them because of my testimony. I don't want to use my liberty as a cloak of maliciousness; that is, I don't want my weaker brother to be hurt by what I do. We must remember that although we are *free*, we are the *servants* of God.[43]

3. Read Romans 6:19-23. How does slavery to sin differ from slavery to righteousness?

4. How have you experienced both freedom and slavery in your relationship with Jesus Christ?

Close out your time today with an open and honest heart before your Maker. Reflect and ask, "To whom or what am I slave? Who or what is my master?"

> *Luis Palau once said, "If you like sin, you'll love holiness." Sin satisfies for a little while. Holiness satisfies forever. Slavery to God frees us to fulfill the destiny for which we were created by God. True freedom is slavery to Christ.[44]*
>
> ~ Keith Krell

Read I Peter 2:17.

Today, we will focus on just one verse – I Peter 2:17. The NLT reads, "Honor all people, love the brotherhood, fear God, honor the king." Underline the second word in the verse above. Other translations read, "Honor all people" and "Show proper respect to everyone." We see a recurring theme no matter the translation...inclusivity for all mankind. Peter does not list conditions or exceptions. A due respect is to be given to all men.

1. Read Genesis 1:27. Why should all people be treated with respect and honor?

2. How different might the world be if we lived by and operated in this truth?

Consider this quote from John Piper. "Give to all human beings (good and bad) a basic respect and honor. The way you respect a scoundrel like Judas and the way you respect a saint like John will be different. But there is a way. And we are to look for it and find it."[45]

3. How can you show honor and respect to others?

4. What about those with whom you disagree or those who have made grievous mistakes?

5. Read the following two verses. How can we apply these principles as we seek to honor and respect others?

Matthew 7:12

Romans 12:10

*If I belittle those whom I am called to serve, talk of their weak points in contrast perhaps with what I think of as my strong points; if I adopt a superior attitude…then I know nothing of Calvary love.*[46]
~ Amy Carmichael

Honoring all people, regardless of skin color, economic status, background, education, etc., is a radical way to *shine* the light of *Jesus* in a dark world.

Honor as taught in Scripture looks very different from honor sought after by the world. Honoring <u>all</u> people, regardless of skin color, economic status, background, education, etc., is a radical way to shine the light of Jesus in a dark world. This week, consider a way to show honor and respect to someone who, by human standards, is unworthy of such treatment. (Consider sharing your experience with your small group.)

Our text today goes on to say, "…and love your Christian brothers and sisters" (NLT). Loving others is a command in Scripture with which we are familiar. Jesus calls us to follow His example to truly and deeply love our Christian brothers and sisters.

6. Read 1 John 2:9-11. Summarize these verses.

R.C. Sproul says, "When we are honest with ourselves, some Christians are easier to love than others. We all find certain people less offensive than others, and as a result, we will gravitate toward those we consider lovable. But Christ does not call us to love only those easy to love. After all, He Himself died for sinners. If we walk in the light we must love all of our fellow believers." [47]

7. Read the following verses. How can we demonstrate love to other Christians?

Romans 12:9-10

1 Corinthians 12:26

Galatians 5:13

Galatians 6:1-2

Hebrews 10:25

In John 13:35, Jesus explained, "Your love for one another will prove to the world that you are my disciples" (NLT).

Think of the power behind this verse. Take a few moments for some self inspection. Examine your heart and consider your brothers and sisters in Christ.

- Can the world watch closely the way you treat others and have <u>proof</u> that you are a follower of Jesus Christ?
- Do you demonstrate honor without reserve?
- Are you ministering to and encouraging fellow believers?
- Do you kick others when they are down or extend a gracious hand to pick them up?

8. Find a specific way this week to show love to a Christian brother or sister. What did you do?

Verse 17 closes with a firm and direct command. Peter reminds us, "Fear God, and respect the king" (NLT). As with many verses in the Bible, I find the ordering of words to be noteworthy. John Piper says, "Godly submission to a government is marked by a fearless fear of God."[48] Out of a reverent fear and awe for our Maker comes a willing and submissive heart to the authorities God has instituted and/or allowed.

If we find ourselves struggling to "honor the king," we may need to consider our fear of the Lord. Unless the laws of our land contradict Scripture, God commands our submission to governing authorities. 1 Peter 2:17 takes it a step further by instructing us to display honor and respect as we obey.

We have all heard (or spoken) the common instruction given to children that says, "Obey the first time, every time, and with a happy heart." God expects the same from His children. This is another way we can be set apart from the world. We can voice disapproval or disagreement, but we have <u>not</u> been given the right to do so in a disrespectful or derogatory fashion.

So, dear follower of Jesus Christ, will you commit to resetting the tone in your social, political, and religious circles by respecting the king? In doing so, you are ultimately respecting THE King of all kings.

Have you ever worked for an employer who was unfair and unkind? I'm sure most of us have experienced this at some point and to some extent in our lives. As I write, my mind reels through circumstances in which I experienced this in my own life. It is not an easy place to be. It can be painful and exhausting, both physically and emotionally. As with all circumstances in life, God has a specific Word for us and a powerful way of refining us in the process.

Read 1 Peter 2:18-20.

The last few words of verse 20 are an attention grabber! The NLT says, "God is pleased with you." The NASB translates, "...this finds favor with God." What a motivation to dive into Scripture and see what causes our Savior to be pleased with us! We all want God to look upon us with favor and pleasure.

Regarding the verses, the Life Application Study Bible explains, "Many Christians were household slaves. It would be easy for them to submit to masters who were gentle and kind, but Peter encouraged loyalty and perseverance even in the face of unjust treatment."[49]

Read the following observations by Bob Deffinbaugh as it relates to today's verses. His thoughts offer an interesting perspective on Peter's words.

> Peter's words in our text, addressed to slaves, are applicable to every Christian. Let me suggest why this is true. The term Peter uses in our text is not restricted only to slaves nor is this the usual word for slaves. Rather, it is a much less common word which may refer to a broader group (member of a household, domestic servants, including freemen as well as slaves). Thus, not only slaves but servants are addressed. Peter speaks more generally in verse 19 as he lays down a more general principle which applies to all believers.

> Peter is instructing the Christian about submission to authority in the context of suffering for the sake of godly conduct. If Peter's teaching applies here, as it does, surely it applies in less difficult circumstances as well.

> Peter does not allow the fact that the slave may be abused to become an excuse for sin, but rather he instructs us to use it as an opportunity to imitate our Lord and Savior, Jesus Christ.

> Let us therefore approach this text as one which speaks clearly and loudly to each of us, trying to learn the joy and privilege which is ours to suffer as servants of our Lord.[50]

As I read Deffinbaugh's thoughts, I began to ponder my past circumstances. They were opportunities to be a recipient of God's favor. Unfortunately, I did not always adopt this perspective in the face of unfair treatment. As the previous quote says, we can experience joy as we suffer. That may sound a bit contradictory, but we should rise to the challenge to walk in obedience to these commands and know the extravagant joy that can come from suffering as a servant of the Lord.

I do not currently work outside the home, but I still have the opportunity to apply these principles to my life. We all do! We all have authorities in our lives. We answer to others in some capacity. Moreover, we are teaching our children/grandchildren/nieces/nephews to deal with authority in their lives by our example.

What about an unfair teacher or coach for your children? What about the head of that committee that deals harshly with you? Do you prefer God's authority over your own ease and comfort? Do you have a pure desire to please Him?

1. Read the following verses. What do these teach us about suffering? What benefit do we receive?

   James 1:2-4


   Psalm 34:19


   Psalm 119:71


   Philippians 3:10-11


2. Look up the following verses. What resources has God given you in the face of suffering?

   2 Timothy 1:2


   2 Timothy 1:7

2 Timothy 1:14



2 Timothy 3:14-15




*Expect suffering—it is inevitable—but don't forget the powerful*
*resource that you have in Christ. Entrust your life to His ever-present care*
*and control. He loves you, and He will help you endure.* [51]
~ Nancy DeMoss Wolgemuth

We all face circumstances that are unfair, unkind and unreasonable. This is part of living in a fallen world. We cannot eliminate those circumstances from our lives, but we can choose how to respond to them. If we respond biblically, we not only please God, but we also may experience seeing others come to Christ by our good example. That's a win-win!

We have spent this week learning how to respect authority, how to live honorably and in freedom, how to respond to unfair treatment and suffering. Under the inspiration of the Holy Spirit, Peter closes this chapter with a beautiful summation.

Follow in Jesus' steps. He is our example.

Read 1 Peter 2:21-25.

As we walk through these closing verses in Chapter 2, consider the topics we've covered this week. Let's take it a step further. Think of the relationship you have with your husband, children, friends, coworkers, ministry partners, etc. On a daily basis, we have choices to make in how we respond to others. Our responses speak volumes.

Watchman Nee says, "Beloved, be assured the Lord pays far more attention to what comes out of your life than what comes out of your mouth. Do not forget that in every contact you make with someone, something comes out of you. It is either the self coming out of your outward man or God Who is flowing forth out of your spirit."[52]

So if we suffer for doing good, suffer due to unfair treatment, or even suffer as a result of our own sin, Jesus Christ has given us a perfect example in how to respond.

1.  Read 1 Peter 2:22. (Read different translations.) How did Jesus respond?

R.C. Sproul makes the following observation:

> Under the heavy pressure of temptation and the potential for suffering for Christ's sake, we often want to lie to ourselves or others so that we can indulge the flesh and not be subject to any real consequences for following Jesus. Yet God calls us to truth—to be honest with ourselves about sin, laying it aside, and to acknowledge before all who can hear that we

are disciples of the Lord and will not put our submission to His authority behind any other allegiance the world offers. Each day we face a choice: Either we can lie to ourselves or others, justifying sins of all kinds, including falsehood, and denying the Master who bought us. Or we can tell the truth, confronting sin and following Christ with boldness. What choice will we make this day? [53]

2.  How can this be applied in our daily lives?

3.  Look at 1 Peter 2:23. What did Jesus do (and not do)?

4.  Romans 12:19 also instructs us in the area of revenge or retaliation. What does Paul tell us here?

5.  Can you think of a time when you walked obediently in this area? Did you see God move on your behalf?

6.  Read 1 Peter 2:24 slowly. Take a moment to be reminded of and reflect upon Jesus' sacrifice on the cross. Summarize, in your own words, Jesus' atonement for you.

Charles Spurgeon says, "The Lord Jesus Christ bore the punishment that was due to us. The offended God stooped from his glory so that he might save those who dared to rebel against his glory. The infinitely glorious Son of God became a sin-bearer. He had pity on us, became one of us, and bore our sins. Let us remember that everything He did for us, He did himself. The heart that was broken for our sins was His heart, and the life given up was His life."[54]

> When we take time to *meditate* on the reality of what Jesus has done for us, it should compel our *hearts* to follow in His steps with complete abandon.

This Savior, this Redeemer, this Sacrifice, this Indescribable Gift. When we take time to meditate on the reality of what Jesus has done for us, it should compel our hearts to follow in His steps with complete abandon. We can never truly repay God for the gift of eternal life, but oh...we can commit to follow in His steps and look to Him as our example for how to live. And then, by the power of the Holy Spirit living in us, we can do it.

As Natalie Grant sings, "How could I repay such a debt except with my life...?"[55]

Perhaps as you've studied our passage this week, you feel incapable or inadequate to do what He's calling you to do. Let's be honest—these are some challenging commands. And most, if not all, are contrary to our human nature. Our flesh does not want to suffer, especially for doing good and following Christ. We do not want to submit to authority with which we disagree. We have a really hard time working under someone who can be unfair and cruel. Peter concludes this chapter with powerful words of encouragement.

We do not have to do this in our own strength! Aren't you relieved? Verse 25 tells us, "But now you have turned to your Shepherd, the Guardian of your souls."

Some versions use the word "Overseer" instead of "Guardian." The Greek word translated as "Overseer" is *episkopos*. R.C. Sproul comments,

> The Apostolic writers use *episkopos* to describe Christ's intense, loving concern and care for His people. It is an image of great tenderness that shows us how Jesus keeps us secure out of His great love for us. He never takes His eyes off us, guaranteeing that our souls will be preserved and that we will fulfill the purposes for which God made us. Our Father has numbered even the hairs on our heads (Matthew 10:26-33), so there is no reason to doubt that He and His Son are concerned with the smallest details of our lives.[56]

He is our Shepherd! He is the Guardian of our souls! He is our Overseer! We can do what He's called us to do because the same power that raised Jesus from the dead lives in us!

As the psalmist reminds us, "The commandments of the LORD are right, bringing joy to the heart" (Psalm 19:8). He is right, His Word is true and we experience joy when we walk in obedience.

# WEEK 5
## With Those We Love

### I PETER 3:1-12

*For the eyes of the Lord are toward the righteous,*
*And His ears attend to their prayer....*
I Peter 3:12a

*When your identity is in the Rock, your identity is rock solid.*[57]
~ Ann Voskamp

Society has blurred the boundary lines of Scripture. Anything goes these days. The first half of 1 Peter 3 specifically calls men and women, husbands and wives and all Christians to fulfill the roles for which God created them. If we do this well, we will experience outrageous hope and extravagant joy!

Will you choose to be a woman in His hand?

## WEEK 5 · DAY ONE

Read I Peter 3:1-3.

Before we begin, I encourage you to complete this week's study, even if you are an unmarried woman. You may be tempted to skim past these pages thinking this week's study is not applicable to your life. God may have plans for you to be married one day. Chances are you know someone who is married. We can all share these truths with other women and pray these verses over them. Perhaps the Lord will use these verses to guide you as you counsel or minister to a married woman. Never underestimate or doubt how God wants to use you or prepare you in advance to fulfill His purposes.

Verse 1 begins with, "In the same way...". This shows us that 1 Peter 3:1 ties right back into the last chapter. (Before you proceed, go back and reread 1 Peter 2:21-25.)

1. What is the first instruction given to wives in 1 Peter 3:1?

Unlike the text from Ephesians 5 where Paul is instructing a Christian wife and Christian husband, in this passage, Peter is speaking to a saved wife married to an unsaved husband. Peter is telling her to accept the authority of her husband (to be submissive) "in the same way" Jesus submitted to the Father's plan. We, as wives, are to follow Jesus' example as we relate and respond to our husbands, even if they are unsaved or not walking closely with the Lord. *(This is not a command to go along with any plan or instruction contrary to Scripture.)

2. If a husband is unsaved or refusing to obey God's Word, how can the submission of his wife affect him?

Bob Deffinbaugh offers this insight into the text.

> Here is the real test. Can the wife trust God to save her husband by her silence? What does Peter mean by the expression "without a word"?
>
> First, Peter surely forbids a wife to nag her husband with the gospel. This can be blatant or subtle, but it is nevertheless something the husband is keenly aware of and strongly resists. Second, Peter forbids debate. Debate is the effort to change another's mind by continually approaching the discussion from a different point of view, by trying any and every line of argument. Third, Peter forbids those subtle forms of persuasion which may produce natural responses but fail to produce supernatural conversion. Jesus warned about carefully prepared presentations of the gospel rather than a reliance upon the Holy Spirit (Luke 21:12-15). [58]

Simply stated, a husband should be able to observe the actions of his wife and conclude that something is different about her, that her behavior is chaste and respectful. This behavior, according to Scripture, will speak more loudly than our verbal words. An unsaved or carnal husband can be won over by observing this type of life.

3.  How can you live a pure and reverent life? Find Scripture to support your answers.

Purity refers to abstaining from sin. If we want to win our husbands to the Lord, we must live in obedience to God. Steven J. Cole says, "She will be morally pure. Her husband won't distrust her because she's a flirt with other men. She won't use deception or dishonesty to try to get her own way. She will learn to handle anger in a biblical way. Her hope will be in God so that she will have a sweet spirit, even toward a difficult husband. He will see Christlikeness in her."[59]

A wife should be reverent toward her husband. Ephesians 5:33 calls her to respect her husband. Moreover, she should live in reverence to her Heavenly Father. A godly wife will live in the fear of God with a reverent awe of who He is. She will recognize that He is Holy and takes sin seriously. If we have a proper reverence for God, we will respect our husbands.

Maybe your husband is not a Christian. Perhaps he is saved but is not walking closely with God. Hopefully, many of you have a godly husband who leads you well and has an intimate relationship with Jesus Christ. Whatever the case may be, take time to inspect your heart and see where the Refiner's fire could do some purifying.

4.  Take a few moments to look in the spiritual mirror. Does what you see make your husband want to follow Jesus Christ?

*God wants to use you in your marriage. Ask Him to give you a*
*loving attitude toward your spouse and to pour out His love*
*through you. It is a prayer God will answer.[60]*
~ Gary Chapman

*Some of you may live with abuse or in excessively unhealthy and destructive conditions in your marriage. At times, it may be inappropriate or even life-threatening for you to apply unquestioningly the principles of submission. For example, if you are being physically or verbally abused, you need to take steps to protect yourself and your children. If you are in that situation, please discerningly seek out biblical counsel from someone who has been trained to help with your specific issue.

Look to the right. Look to the left. We are surrounded! Beauty tips. Fashion trends. All the how-to's we can possibly stand. As with most societal standards, the world's idea of beauty is fiercely different from God's Word.

According to our Scripture today, our primary concern should not be our outward, physical beauty. We should be focused on the "within." Just as God said to Samuel, "For the LORD DOES NOT SEE AS MAN SEES; FOR MAN LOOKS AT THE OUTWARD APPEARANCE, BUT THE LORD LOOKS AT THE HEART" (1 SAMUEL 16:7, NKJV).

Read 1 Peter 3:4-6.

Imagine standing before the Lord right now. Face to face, eye to eye. If you asked Him, "Lord, what is precious to you?" according to 1 Peter 3:4, His response would be, "...the unfading beauty of a gentle and quiet spirit."

God is not looking for flawless skin. He is looking for a flawless heart.

What is a gentle and quiet spirit? Mary Kassian describes quiet like this:

> When the Bible talks about quietness, it's not referring to an absence of verbal noise as much as it's referring to an absence of spiritual noise. Although there's a connection, quietness has more to do with the state of our hearts than the quantity and volume of our words.
>
> Quiet describes a mindset of calmness, serenity, and tranquility. It's being settled, steadfast, and peaceful. A quiet disposition is like a still, peaceful pool of water, as opposed to a churning, agitated whirlpool. A quiet spirit is the opposite of an anxious, distressed, disorderly, and clamorous one.[61]

1.  Read the following verses. What do you learn about "quietness?"

    Psalm 131:1-3


    Isaiah 30:15


    Isaiah 32:17

Meekness is not weakness. It is Holy Spirit controlled strength. When we are quiet and have a gentle spirit, we extinguish our selfish tendencies. In other words, we allow the Holy Spirit to control our minds and hearts.

2. How can we practically pursue a gentle and quiet spirit?

3. What kind of beauty comes as a result of a gentle and quiet spirit (v. 4)?

4. Read 1 Peter 3:5-6. How did the "holy women of old" make themselves beautiful?

> When we set aside pride and self, we are truly *beautiful* to the One who matters.

Let's be honest. Most of us would love to find a beauty product that could promise unfading, imperishable beauty for our physical bodies. (My hand is up!) Unfortunately, there is no such product out there for our outward appearance. However, God tells us that the beauty that comes from within is not only precious in His sight, but it is also lasting! Unlike our physical beauty, it will not fade. It will not grow old and be no more.

This should delight our hearts more than any promise the world has to offer to make us beautiful. Any physical makeover will have to be repeated to achieve the desired results. A Holy Spirit makeover is a one time thing! Yes, we must go before Him daily to be filled and renewed, but what He does in our hearts lasts! The beauty that comes from a surrendered life is fulfilling and lasting.

5. As you meditate and reflect on the Scripture today, what changes need to be made in your heart so that you reflect a gentle and quiet spirit, one that is precious in the sight of the Lord?

When we set aside pride and self, we are truly beautiful to the One who matters.

*Meekness is calm confidence, settled assurance, and rest of the soul. It is the tranquil stillness of a heart that is at rest in Christ. It is the place of peace. Meekness springs from a heart of humility, radiating the fragrance of Christ.* [62]
~ Kimberly Wagner

# WEEK 5 · DAY THREE
## I PETER 3:7

I must admit a bit of hesitancy as I begin to pen the words for today's study. How do I relay a message to women and make it applicable when the text is specifically addressed to husbands? As I pondered this for several days, the Lord spoke these words to my heart:

"Share the truths from My Word. Encourage women to pray accordingly."

Are you married? Do you have a married son? Are you hoping to be married one day? Are you raising boys? Do you have grandsons? Do you or your family have influence over a young man? Have you found yourself in difficult conversations with people who do not have a biblical perspective on marriage? I am certain all of us can answer "yes" to at least one of these questions.

Before we dive into 1 Peter 3:7, ask the Lord for fresh eyes to see the truths in this verse. Ask Him to reveal to your heart how He would like to use this verse specifically in your life today. As a woman, what will you do with this Scripture that is directed toward husbands?

Read I Peter 3:7.

1.  How should husbands treat their wives (list two ways)?

2.  Why is the wife to be treated with honor (list two reasons)?

A woman should be treated with honor because she is the weaker vessel. Peter was "not implying moral or intellectual inferiority, but was recognizing women's physical limitations. A man who honors his wife as a member of the weaker sex will protect, respect, help, and stay with her. He will be sensitive to her needs, and he will relate to her with courtesy, consideration, insight, and tact."[63]

3. What are some practical ways a husband can show this type of honor to his wife? (If you are married, what are some things your husband does that make you feel special and honored?)

Sometimes, we, as women, can get a little testy over the subject of submission. It is often hard, even though we know it is God's order for the family. Let us consider today the role of husbands, and the consequences thereof, as we look at the last part of this verse.

This verse closes with a powerful punch, a high calling and a most serious consequence if disobeyed.

4. What is the result if a husband does not treat his wife as he should?

J. Vernon McGee says, "It will ruin your family altar."[64] Does that not grab your attention?

5. As a woman, how can you take this packed verse and apply it to your life today?

*Married Women:*

Pray these verses over your husband regularly. If he is doing these things well, thank the Lord for this (and thank your husband often) and ask Him to keep your husband surrendered in these areas. If your husband is not doing this well, ask the Holy Spirit to convict him and speak to his heart specifically about living with you in understanding and honoring you as his wife. Consider asking a trusted friend to pray alongside you.

*Unmarried Women* (hoping to someday be married):

Ask the Lord for a husband who knows and fears the Lord and takes these commands seriously. Have conversations prior to marriage about what God's Word says to both husbands and wives. If you are involved with a man who is harsh and does not treat you with honor and care, consider discontinuing the relationship under these terms.

*Moms of Boys:*

Begin early to teach your boys what manhood looks like. Show them what God's Word says about how they should one day treat a wife. Point out those moments when your husband shows honor and special care toward you. Pray now for God to etch these truths onto their hearts, that they will be tender and responsive to God's way rather than the world's way.

6. In addition to these suggestions, what are other ways women can use and/or apply this verse?

I want to close today with observations from J. Vernon McGee on this section of Scripture relating to husbands and wives:

> Scripture says that God took man and from man He made woman. Using the Hebrew words, Genesis 2:23 reads, "She shall be called *Isha*, because she was taken out of *Ish*." She is called "...a help *meet* for him" (Genesis 2:18); that is, a help that was fit for him. In other words, she was to be the other half of him. He was only half a man, and she was to be the other part of him. With that in mind, you can see that the marriage relationship is not to be one of a man insisting on treating his wife like a little child who has to jump every time he says so. She is there to *help* him. She is there to be a *part* of him. She is there to *love* him. And he is there to *love* and *protect* her. That is the ideal relationship in marriage.[65]

No matter your place in life, God can use this instruction to husbands to shape and form your idea of Christian marriage. You can, in turn, use this to help others and to pray for the men God has placed in your life.

Unity. This can be a foreign concept in today's society. Families. Cultures. Churches. Politics. Races. Division has become commonplace in these facets of life. Sadly, for many of us, we have grown complacent and have accepted this as a way of life.

Our text today is polar opposite from this all too common point of view. As Christians, we are called to be set apart, to look different than the world around us.

Before we begin, honestly inspect your heart and mind. Where do you see division in your life? Is your family divided? Do you view another race as less significant than you? Do you struggle joining hands with other believers if they belong to a different denomination? Is it difficult to associate with a person who holds a political opinion different than yours? Do you grumble and complain if a song or sermon doesn't suit your taste?

If any of these are true of you, stop and confess it to the Lord. Ask Him to use His Word to penetrate the crevices in your heart where you have allowed divisive thoughts to fester.

Read 1 Peter 3:8-9.

My church has long been praying for spiritual awakening in our city and nation. A common phrase we associate with this prayer is "It starts in me." I thought of this as I read 1 Peter 3:8-9. Peter is speaking to Christians. We must be trailblazers in these areas, encouraging other believers as well as setting an example for the lost world around us.

1.  Read John 13:35. How will the world know we are Christ followers?

It starts in me. It starts in you. It starts in us. We are able to show and share the truth of the gospel if we, as Christians, love one another. Let's see how we can practically live this out.

2. Read 1 Peter 3:8-9. List the five key elements that should characterize any group of believers.

3. Let us look at the Greek word for the qualities God desires to see in His church. For each of these, jot down your thoughts on how we can walk in obedience to these verses.

   a. *homophrōn* – pertaining to, being like-minded, united in spirit, harmonious. What about the things on which we disagree?

   b. *sympathēs* – sympathetic, understanding. Read Galatians 6:2 for additional insight.

   c. *philadelphos* – loving one's brother/sister. How can we show love as a family?

   d. *eusplanchnos* – pertaining to, having tender feelings for someone, kind hearted, compassionate

   e. *tapeinophrōn* – humble, modest

Consider this commentary from the Life Application Study Bible,

> God chose Peter and others to show what a difference true faith makes in the real world. So here the once rash, belligerent, domineering and arrogant Peter bears witness to a life of harmony, compassion, love and humility. What a difference God makes! You, too, are God's witness to skeptical people. Let your life be evidence of God's truth. Let your pride become humility and your insensitivity give way to genuine affection for others.[66]

It is often deemed acceptable to get back at those who have hurt us. Our sinful nature longs to seek revenge. For Christians, revenge is never the right option.

4.  How are we to respond when someone hurts us or sins against us (v. 9a)?

5.  What does the Bible say about seeking revenge or repaying evil for evil?

    Matthew 5:38-39

    1 Thessalonians 5:15

    Proverbs 20:22

    Romans 12:19

6. Look at the last part of I Peter 3, verse 9. Rather than repaying evil for evil, what are we commanded to do?

7. This command has a promise attached to it. What will God do if we pay back with a blessing?

What a stark contrast to the secular worldview! You do not want to miss the promises of God. 2 Corinthians 1:20 tells us, "For no matter how many promises God has made, they are 'Yes' in Christ" (NIV).

Recently, I have had to help one of my children walk through difficult circumstances that required making a choice in how to respond. There is no pain quite like seeing your child hurt as a result of another's unkindness. How do we (as parents, grandparents, role models, influences), teach and lead others to respond in a Christ-like manner?

In these instances, I've told my child to pray for the offender. (I also had to remind myself of this as my heart hurt and I felt anger toward the ones that had hurt him.) God's Word tells us to pay back with a blessing. I cannot think of a better blessing to offer someone than to carry them to the Throne Room of Heaven in prayer.

Has someone hurt you? Has someone hurt a member of your family? Resist the temptation to pay them back as the world sees fit. Instead, take them to the One who has experienced suffering and pain far beyond what we can ever imagine. Jesus Christ was betrayed, tortured and crucified...none of which He deserved. He carried the weight of all our sin, and as He did, He prayed that God would forgive those who hurt Him.

Let us follow His example. How well do you love Jesus? How well do you love others?

*He said "Love...as I have loved you." We cannot love too much.*[67]
~ Amy Carmichael

Peter quotes from Psalm 34 in today's text. 1 Peter 3:10 begins with an "if" statement. Anytime Scripture begins this way, we should make note of it. God's "if" statements are powerful and poignant and worthy of our attention.

He says, "If you want to enjoy life and see many happy days…"(NLT). An enjoyable life filled with happiness is appealing to all of mankind. If we truly want to experience this, we must study and apply Peter's formula.

Read 1 Peter 3:10-12.

1.   List the conditions that lead to an enjoyable life and happy days.

Watch your toes! For most women, the tongue can be a touchy subject. The Bible tells us, "The tongue has the power of life and death" (Proverbs 18:21, NIV). I find it interesting that our words are the first item addressed in experiencing an enjoyable life. We sometimes fall into the trap of believing our words carry little weight. This is a lie of the enemy.

2.   Read James 3:2-18 to be reminded of the power of the tongue. How can you apply these principles in your daily life (and teach them to your children/grandchildren/those over whom you have influence)?

One of my favorite (and most convicting) quotes from Amy Carmichael is this:

> "If a sudden jar can cause me to speak an impatient, unloving word, then I know nothing of Calvary love. For a cup brimful of sweet water cannot spill even one drop of bitter water, however suddenly jolted."[68]

What type of water is spilling out of your cup?

The Scripture goes on to say, "Turn away from evil and do good" (v. 11). Job is described in this way, "...blameless, upright, fearing God and turning away from evil" (Job 1:1). Job was not perfect or without sin (only Jesus was), but is consistently described as a man of integrity.

We never stand still spiritually. We are either moving towards sin or away from it.

3.  According to 2 Timothy 2:22, what must we run from and what must we run to?

4.  How can you walk in obedience to this verse and follow Job's example of turning away from evil? How would you encourage others to do the same? Search the Scripture to support your answers.

Our world is full of unrest. It seems peace can be hard to find. As Christ-followers, we are commanded to search for it and then work to maintain it.

I love the Amplified Bible translation which says, "He must search for peace [with God, with self, with others] and pursue it eagerly [actively—not merely desiring it]" (1 Peter 3:11b). This calls for action on our part. Wanting peace is not enough. We must search for and pursue peace, not just have a desire for it.

5. Read the following verses. How can you actively and eagerly pursue peace with God, yourself, and others?

Romans 12:18

Isaiah 26:3

Proverbs 16:7

This passage of Scripture wraps up with another beautiful promise.

6. What blessings do we receive if we do right (1 Peter 3:12)?

Can you think of a more treasured gift than the eyes of the Lord watching over you and the ears of the Lord open to your prayers?  This, my dear sister, will result in outrageous hope and extravagant joy!

Close today's study with the following prayer:

> Heavenly Father, strengthen me to do my part to be of one mind with other believers. Help me to sympathize with others, to love others as my own family, to be tenderhearted and keep a humble attitude. I pray I never repay evil for evil but rather pay it back with a blessing. I desire to do what You have called me to do and to experience Your blessing for doing it. I want to enjoy life and see many happy days, so help me to control my tongue by never speaking lies or speaking evil. Give me Your strength to turn away from evil and do good. Help me to actively search for peace and to passionately work to maintain it. I want nothing more than for Your eyes to watch over me and for Your ears to be open to my prayers. Thank You for the promises in Your Word. In Jesus' name I pray, Amen.

> *Let's live it up, my friend, but let's not live it up by indulging in gossip and evil.*
> *Let's live it up by turning away from evil and pursuing that which ministers to peace.*
> *Let's live for God today. How important this is!*[69]
> ~ J. Vernon McGee

# WEEK 6
## Despite a Hostile World

### 1 PETER 3:13-22

*But sanctify Christ as Lord in your hearts.*
1 Peter 3:15a

*Allow God to strengthen you by His Spirit in the inner man, that the Lord Jesus may be glorified in your heart as He is glorified in heaven—then the river will flow, and make glad the city of God.*[70]
~ Major W. Ian Thomas

We begin a new week in our study with the words of Peter ringing in our ears and our hearts full of the truth that he shared in his letter to the believers in Asia Minor. We have contemplated our eternal inheritance based on the sufficiency of Jesus' sacrifice. We have reflected on the call to personal holiness and godly living. Jesus has been exalted as our example in the midst of trials and persecution. And this week we will ponder the prescription for walking triumphantly despite a world that is becoming increasingly hostile to Christianity.

Thanks to the religious liberty built into our Constitution by our Founding Fathers, Christians in the United States have not suffered like the early believers and Christians down through the centuries who encountered trial after trial because of their faith. Yet now we see the tide of culture changing for those in our country who take their faith seriously. It takes the form of criticism, ridicule, and sometimes outright hostility. This should be expected because we are not of this world, and we do not think as the world thinks. However, much depends on how we respond to persecution—the lost world is watching. So, let's delve right in to see the advice that Peter, through the inspiration of the Holy Spirit, gives us as we face the trials that are sure to come.

Read 1 Peter 3:13-14.

Peter begins this passage by asking a rhetorical question for his readers to consider.

1.  What is Peter's rhetorical question in verse 13?

2.  While Peter seems to infer that one will not suffer if one does good, what does he say by way of encouragement to those who do suffer in verse 14?

Tucked within the text of verse 14 is a quote from Isaiah 8 that Peter uses to reassure persecuted believers: "And do not fear their intimidation, and do not be troubled." The background for this quote is found in 2 Kings 16 and Isaiah 7. Ahaz, King of Judah, was in the midst of a crisis facing invasion by the forces of Israel and Aram. Ahaz and the people of Judah were terrified. The Lord sent the prophet Isaiah to calm them with the promise that what they feared would not transpire. Ahaz was warned by Isaiah not to engage in unholy alliances, but rather to trust in the Lord. Unfortunately, Ahaz, who did not walk closely with the Lord, did not heed Isaiah's instruction, but made an alliance with Assyria—and the consequences were grave.

Read 2 Kings 16:7-18.

3. What were the results of Ahaz forming an alliance with Assyria? What assumptions would you make concerning the impact of Ahaz's decision on the nation of Judah?

4. How does Peter describe the person who suffers for righteousness sake?

Jesus encourages the persecuted in much the same way in the Sermon on the Mount.

5. What specifics does Jesus enumerate concerning those who are persecuted in Matthew 5:10-12?

*The New Bible Commentary* sums up what we have been discussing beautifully:

> Persecution may well come upon the Christian, but it cannot ultimately do injury. In fact the experience can lead to blessing and the outcome can be left in God's hands as He watches over His own and their persecutors. So believers are urged not to be frightened.[71]

6. Remind yourself of the power and protection available to us in our great God as you read these familiar verses. Record what is a comfort to you.

Deuteronomy 31:6

Psalm 27:1

John 14:27


Jude 1:24


Today, I would like for us to examine the testimony of a wonderful woman who served God by faithfully doing good, yet she was persecuted. Her name was Dr. Helen Roseveare, and she served as a medical missionary in what was then known as the Congo. She ran a hospital with 100 beds that served women, children, and lepers. Additionally, she developed a training school for paramedics and 48 rural clinics. Her heart was deeply invested in the people of the Congo. But then civil war erupted in the Congo in 1964 and all of the facilities were destroyed. Helen was arrested and imprisoned along with other missionaries. Here is her account of what happened after her attempt to escape:

> They found me, dragged me to my feet, struck me over head and shoulders, flung me on the ground, kicked me, dragged me to my feet only to strike me again—the sickening searing pain of a broken tooth, a mouth full of sticky blood, my glasses gone. Beyond sense, numb with horror and unknown fear, driven, dragged, pushed back to my own house—yelled at, insulted, cursed.

> Her captors, she wrote, were brutal and drunken. They cursed and swore, they struck and kicked, they used the butt-end of rifles and rubber truncheons. We were roughly taken, thrown in prisons, humiliated, threatened.

On October 29, 1964, Helen Roseveare was brutally raped.

She later recounted:

> On that dreadful night, beaten and bruised, terrified and tormented, unutterably alone, I had felt at last God had failed me. Surely He could have stepped in earlier, surely things need not have gone that far. I had reached what seemed to be the ultimate depth of despairing nothingness.

In this darkness, however, she sensed the Lord saying to her:

> You asked Me, when you were first converted, for the privilege of being a missionary. This is it. Don't you want it? These are not your sufferings. They're Mine. All I ask of you is the loan of your body.

She later pointed to God's goodness despite this great evil:

> Through the brutal heartbreaking experience of rape, God met with me—with outstretched arms of love. It was an unbelievable experience: He was so utterly there, so totally understanding, His comfort was so complete—and suddenly I knew—I really knew that His love was unutterably sufficient. He did love me! He did understand!

One word became unbelievably clear, and that word was privilege. He didn't take away pain or cruelty or humiliation. No! It was all there, but now it was altogether different. It was with Him, for Him, in Him. He was actually offering me the inestimable privilege of sharing in some little way the edge of the fellowship of his suffering.[72]

Enemies may hurt us, but nothing can truly harm us. We are secure in Christ our Savior!

*God never uses a person greatly until He has wounded him deeply.*
*The privilege He offers you is greater than the price you have to pay.*
*The privilege is greater than the price.[73]*
~ Helen Roseveare

*Enemies may hurt us, but nothing can truly harm us. We are secure in Christ our Savior!*

In our study today, we will simply focus on the first phrase in 1 Peter 3:15, "But sanctify Christ as Lord in your hearts." Just what does it denote to sanctify Christ as Lord? According to the *Hebrew-Greek Key Word Study Bible*, the Greek word, *hagiazo*, means "to sanctify, set apart, make holy."[74] A further explanation from this reference says, "To regard as holy, treat as holy, revere, venerate, hallow; of God's name, His character, the sum of His person as God."[75]

In order to comprehend exactly what it means to sanctify or set apart Jesus Christ as Lord in our hearts, a glimpse into the life of Esther Ahn Kim will serve to enlighten us.

Leslie Ludy tells Kim's story:

> Esther Ahn Kim walked slowly up the hill to the shrine, with her students following silently behind her. The young music teacher knew that when she arrived at the place of worship she would be forced to make a life-altering choice. The Japanese, who had taken control of Korea two years prior in 1937, were forcing everyone to bow at the shrine of their 'sun god.' The punishment for refusing was imprisonment, torture, and possibly even death.

> At that moment, Esther knew what she would do. Even though so many other Christians had decided that outwardly bowing to the idol was acceptable as long as they continued to worship Christ in their hearts, Esther could make no such compromise. She would not bow to any other but the one true God.

> 'Attention!' came the commanding voice of one of the officials. The crowd stood in silent submission. 'Our profoundest bow to Amaterasu Omikami!' As he shouted the words, the entire group bent the upper half of their bodies, bowing solemnly before the shrine. Esther was the only one who remained standing, looking up at the sky. The fear and uncertainty that had gripped her just moments before had vanished. Calmness and peace flooded her. She had done what she knew God wanted her to do.

> Her courageous stand for Christ led to six harrowing years in Japanese prisons. During that time, though her body grew weak with suffering, she shone with supernatural love toward her persecutors and fellow prisoners. Even through torture, she refused to deny the name of Christ. Her astounding example of 'suffering hardship as a good soldier for Christ' brought many into the kingdom who would never have heard the gospel otherwise.[76]

I remember sitting at a women's conference and listening as Esther Ahn Kim shared her story of these harrowing experiences. It was a moment I will never forget. Truly this brave and faithful woman set apart Jesus as Lord in her heart. I am challenged by her faith. Are you?

1. From your perspective, what does it mean to sanctify Christ as Lord in your heart?

2. What did Jesus tell His disciples about the cost of making Him preeminent in their hearts in the following passages?

   Luke 9:23-25

   Matthew 10:38

As women, we can become very distracted with all of our responsibilities vying for our attention. Sometimes our hearts can become distant and even grow cold toward our Lord, denying Him the exalted position in our hearts. Jesus focused on this possibility in His interaction with Martha.

3. How did Jesus address Martha's complaint in Luke 10:38-42? What did He encourage her to do?

4. Meditate on what Jesus has done for you that should give Him that preeminent place in your heart. Chronicle what comes to your mind and touches your heart.

5. Scripture is replete with knowledge concerning the heart. Record what you discover in these verses.

Proverbs 21:2

James 4:8

Psalm 112:7

In The New American Commentary, Thomas Schreiner comments:

> The heart is the origin of human behavior, and from it flows everything people do. Hence, setting apart Christ as Lord in the heart is not merely a private reality but will be evident to all when believers suffer for their faith. The inner and outer life are inseparable, for what happens within will inevitably be displayed to all, especially when one suffers.[77]

This was certainly the case in the testimony of Esther Ahn Kim. People recognized her heart's commitment to Jesus Christ. It spoke volumes to them. Many responded in faith.

6. What steps will you take to ensure that Christ is Lord in your heart?

Leslie Ludy concluded her blog about Esther Ahn Kim in this manner:

> This world needs more women like Esther Ahn Kim—women who unreservedly take up their cross and follow Him, no matter what the cost. May it be our greatest desire to follow such a path and joyfully suffer any hardship for the One who gave everything for us. The world will never be the same when they encounter such a life.[78]

My friend, guard your heart.

*Above all else, guard your heart, for it is the wellspring of life.*
Proverbs 4:23

In our study yesterday, we were challenged to "sanctify Christ as Lord in your hearts" (1 Peter 3:15a). Indeed, this is exceedingly crucial for Christ followers as we navigate life in a hostile world, where we are to be salt and light to those we meet on our journey. Today we will focus on the second half of verse 15 where Peter urged the believers to be bold in their witness for Jesus Christ.

Read I Peter 3:15.

1. What does Peter encourage the Christians to do in 1 Peter 3:15b? When?

We are to be equipped to give a defense, explanation, or apology of our faith to anyone who inquires—to share the hope or expectation of our great salvation. Yet to do so necessitates a life that is noticeably different from that of the world.

> We are to be equipped to give a defense, explanation, or apology of our *faith* to anyone who inquires—to share the *hope* or expectation of our great salvation.

2. Meditate on this question and ask the Lord to give you insight. Does your life look distinctively different from the world?

3. Do you recall a time when someone asked you to give a reason for the hope within you? Relate the circumstances. If not, compose a prayer entreating the Lord for an opportunity to share your faith.

The theological discipline of defending the faith is called apologetics which rests on truth as revealed to us in God's Word. Christian apologist, Mary Jo Sharp, offers the following definition: *"Apologetics*—a Koine Greek word, transliterated from the New Testament text. It means *to give or make a defense.* In the context of my field of study, the word means specifically to make a case for belief in the Christian God, which includes answering objections to belief in God."[79]

In today's culture, however, truth is often waived in favor of tolerance when religion is considered. An article from the New York Times regarding a Pew survey from a few years ago is enlightening regarding the beliefs of Christians today. This excerpt will clarify the deviation from truth:

> Although a majority of Americans say religion is very important to them, nearly three-quarters of them say they believe that many faiths beside their own can lead to salvation, according to a survey by the Pew Forum on Religion and Public Life. The report, the U. S. Religious Landscape Survey, reveals a broad trend toward tolerance and an ability among many Americans to hold beliefs that might contradict the doctrines of their professed faiths.

> For example, 70 percent of Americans affiliated with a religion or denomination said they agreed that "many religions can lead to eternal life," including majorities among Protestants and Catholics. Among evangelical Christians, 57 percent agreed with the statement, and among Catholics, 79 percent did.[80]

Mary Jo Sharp clears up the confusion regarding tolerance: "Real tolerance is not about the equality of all beliefs or religions or ideologies. Tolerance is about the equality of people despite our disagreements with various beliefs and religions and ideologies."[81]

In order to give a defense for our hope, we must be able to confidently articulate the non-negotiable truths of authentic Christianity.

4.  Make a list of what you would consider to be the non-negotiable doctrines of Christianity.

5. Review the Scriptures listed on the chart. Record the key doctrinal truth revealed in each. Check to see if your list in question 4 coincides with this one.

| SCRIPTURE | DOCTRINAL TRUTH |
|---|---|
| 2 Timothy 3:16 | |
| Romans 1:3-4 | |
| Romans 3:23 | |
| John 14:6 | |
| Philippians 2:8 | |
| Acts 2:24 | |
| Acts 2:38 | |
| Matthew 25:31 | |

Are you prepared to share your faith? Are you confident? Have some elements of cultural thinking flawed your theological discernment? Does your life cause others to ask you about your hope?

Mary Jo Sharp gives some insight: "Some Christians appear to have laid a foundation of salvation in Jesus Christ, but seem to construct the house of their lives upon the shifting ground of worldly culture. Hearing the Word of God and acknowledging it as true is different from obeying the Word and constructing your life upon it."[82]

6. What two key ingredients does Peter recommend you display when you share your faith?

7. What understanding do you discover in Colossians 4:5-6 to assist you as you share?

When I was in college, I spent one summer in Ohio and Michigan working for the Home Mission Board of the Southern Baptist Convention (now the North American Mission Board). One of my first assignments was to canvas a neighborhood in a large city by taking a religious survey. I encountered various reactions to my knock on the door—doors slammed in my face, disinterest, the recounting of some very interesting theological opinions, etc. One afternoon I stepped upon the porch of a duplex and tapped on the first door. An older woman answered and emphatically responded that she was not interested in spiritual things and closed the door. I moved on to the next duplex unit where a young woman with children at her side responded and invited me in. As she replied to my questions, the woman from next door entered through the back door. My immediate thought was that this opportunity to share the gospel had come to an end. But rather than usher me out, she simply said, "I used to go to church when I was a girl." And the conversation began.

I discovered that afternoon that there is indeed "a God-shaped vacuum" in every heart. That mother and daughter listened very carefully to my presentation and later I learned that they both made a profession of faith and began attending the local Baptist church. People long to know about the hope that is in you.

*Always being ready to make a defense to everyone who asks you to give an*
*account for the hope that is in you, yet with gentleness and reverence.*
1 Peter 3:15b

# WEEK 6 · DAY FOUR

## 1 PETER 3:16-17

The challenge from our study yesterday was to be equipped and confident to give a reason for the hope of our salvation to those we meet as we journey through a fallen world. Next, Peter revisits a recurring theme in this letter to the believers in Asia Minor—suffering and persecution—and communicates some applicable advice in light of the probability of the suffering to come.

Read I Peter 3:16-17.

1. What advice does Peter impart to the believers in 1 Peter 3:16?

The Greek word *syneidesis* means conscience. "It denotes that faculty of the mind whose nature it is to bear witness to one's own moral conduct. Particularly, self-knowledge, consciousness; and hence, conscience, that which distinguishes between right and wrong, and prompts to choose the former and avoid the latter."[83]

After having denied Jesus three times prior to his crucifixion, the memory of a guilty conscience must have been clear in Peter's mind. He knew the relief of forgiveness and the importance of a clear conscience between God and man.

2. Investigate these verses and describe the types of consciences depicted.

   Titus 1:15

   1 Timothy 4:1-2

   Hebrews 10:22

3. As members of sinful, fallen humankind, how can we have a good conscience before God? Review Hebrews 10:22 again along with Hebrews 9:14 and record your answer.

Warren Wiersbe offers some insight concerning conscience:

> Conscience may be compared to a window that lets in the light of God's truth. If we persist in disobeying, the window gets dirtier and dirtier, until the light cannot enter. Conscience depends on knowledge, the "light" coming through the window. As a believer studies the Word, he better understands the will of God, and his conscience becomes more sensitive to right and wrong. A "good conscience" is one that accuses when we think or do wrong and approves when we do right.[84]

4. Read I John 1:5-7. How would you correlate these verses with the ability to have a clear conscience?

5. When Paul appeared before Governor Felix, what goal does he mention in Acts 24:16 which we should desire, as well?

6. What reasoning does Peter use in verse 16 to justify the need for a good conscience?

7.  In 1 Peter 3:17, what reference do you see to God's permissive will?

Peter encouraged the believers to walk righteously in their world, keeping a good conscience before God and man. Then if God allowed suffering to arise in their lives, it would be undeserved for doing what is right. The Biblical narrative incorporates many such instances through which we can obtain encouragement and perception for what might await us in the future. Let's look at a few familiar yet powerful illustrations of God's presence in the midst of suffering despite doing good.

8.  Read these passages and record what you discover about suffering or about the character and presence of God in its midst.

| | |
|---|---|
| Joseph – Genesis 50:14-21 | |
| Elijah – I Kings 19:2-15 | |
| Daniel – Daniel 6:16-23 | |
| Mary – Luke 1:26-38 | |

Throughout the centuries and in our world today, God's people have suffered as a result of their faith. In the last few years, we have seen the news reports from the Middle East and Africa of beheadings by ISIS, bombings at Christian churches, kidnappings of young girls, etc. Our hearts break, yet we seem so far removed from the persecution. So much so, that I fear that we forget their plight and do not continually lift up our fellow believers to the Lord nor seek ways to meet their needs. Let us not assume that our country will be spared. We can believe, however, that if persecution comes, our God will never forsake us.

As we conclude our study today, I want to share the example of an Iraqi couple, Muslim by birth, who met the Lord Jesus Christ through the testimony of Christians and the appearance of Christ through dreams—which happens frequently in the Muslim world. Their names are Shukri and Khadija and this is their story:

> Shortly after their salvation, they felt compelled to move to Mosul to share their faith, where an imam unbelievably gave Shukri permission to distribute Bibles at the door of the Great Mosque. One morning during his prayer time, Shukri had the distinct impression that it was the day he would see the Lord. Nevertheless, he was not deterred in his determination to again hand out Bibles at the mosque. And so, he did. As he left six men surrounded him. He smiled. 'I am a messenger from the Lord Jesus Christ.' The man who had grabbed Shukri pulled a *jambiya* from under his garment. Sunlight flared off the blade, and the man smiled back. 'We are from ISIS.'[85]

Here is the testimony of Shukri's faithful wife, Khadija, following his death:

> The hardest thing to talk about, though, is how cruelly ISIS tortured Shukri before he died. They slashed him with knives all over his body before shooting him at least ten times in the head and chest. They dragged him off and buried him in a patch of sand.

> The police called me to the scene to identify Shukri's body, and when I arrived, they had already pulled him out of the shallow grave. They showed me the note ISIS had pinned to Shukri's shirt and told me that when they found him, Shukri's right hand was sticking out of the ground and pointing toward heaven. Only one thing helped me bear the sight of my dear Shukri, sprawled on the ground, bloody, beaten, and lifeless: he was smiling.[86]

Take a few moments right now to pray for persecuted Christians around the world. We may lose our lives, but no harm will befall us for we have a Living Hope and an imperishable inheritance!

Yesterday, we considered Peter's directive for believers to exist with a good conscience toward God and men while reminding them that suffering for doing right far surpassed the suffering for doing wrong. We also reflected on the lives of a few of our Biblical heroes who faced seemingly underserved suffering. However, in our study passage today, 1 Peter 3:18-22, the Lord Jesus Christ is pictured as the perfect example of underserved suffering. 2 Corinthians 5:21 renders it so succinctly: "He made Him who knew no sin to be sin on our behalf, so that we might become the righteousness of God in Him."

Read 1 Peter 3:18-22.

1.  Name five important facets listed in 1 Peter 3:18 regarding Christ's atonement on our behalf.

2.  What additional benefits can you find and attribute to the salvation you possess through Christ Jesus in these verses?

    Romans 5:1

    Colossians 1:22

    Ephesians 3:12

    Hebrews 9:11-14

    Hebrews 10:19

*The New Bible Commentary* describes the sufferings of Jesus so aptly when it says: "The one person whose perfect righteousness meant that He never deserved to die endured the pains of death on behalf of all who did deserve to die. In this way Jesus took our place and endured our punishment."[87]

3.  Upon contemplation of Jesus' sacrifice for you, what is your response?

Much debate swirls around the next verses (vv. 19-20) among theologians. Peter states that Jesus Christ made a proclamation to spirits in prison which raises several questions. Who were these spirits? Where and when did Jesus make his proclamation? What did He proclaim to them? Several explanations have been given by commentators regarding this passage, but there does not appear to be a consensus. Martin Luther summarizes the commentary well, "A wonderful text is this, and a more obscure passage perhaps than any other in the New Testament, so that I do not know for a certainty just what Peter means."[88]

To thoroughly investigate this passage would require extensive study, so let's consider a short explanation from *The Woman's Study Bible:*

> The spirits in prison could refer to evil angels, to individuals who have died, or to the people who were alive at the time of Noah (v. 19). The passage is difficult to interpret. Christ apparently preached to these "spirits" after His death and before His Resurrection, or perhaps He preached through Noah to the antediluvians prior to the flood (v. 22). The content of Christ's message was likely a victorious proclamation of the defeat of the enemies of God. Peter mentioned this because he wanted the suffering Christians to know that one day their persecutors would face this condemning proclamation just like the evil spirits of the days of Noah.[89]

Some theologians have suggested that Christ actually went into hell to offer the unsaved a second chance for salvation. This view, however, is a direct contradiction to Scripture.

4. What substantiation do you find in Hebrews 9:27 for the concept that there is no second chance opportunity for salvation after death?

In verses 20-21, Peter compares the water deliverance of Noah and his family with baptism. On first reading, it might appear that Peter is saying that baptism is necessary for salvation, but a closer examination of verse 21 reveals that baptism is "not the removal of dirt from the flesh, but an appeal to God for a good conscience" (I Peter 3:21). *The Bible Knowledge Commentary* expounds on baptism: "Baptism represents a complete break with one's past life. As the Flood wiped away the old sinful world, so baptism pictures one's break from his old sinful life and his entrance into a new life in Christ."[90]

As we approach the climax of the chapter, we have reason to rejoice over our great Savior. Death could not hold Him in its grip. He is the triumphant God Man Who has secured our salvation.

5. Why was Jesus' resurrection from the dead so crucial to our salvation?

6. According to verse 22, where is Jesus presently?

7. What do these Scriptures convey that Jesus is doing on our behalf in Heaven?

Romans 8:34

1 Timothy 2:15

Hebrews 7:25


1 John 2:1


Our study for this week has come to an end. We have contemplated suffering in the life of a Christian, what it means to truly set apart Jesus as Lord in our hearts, the depths of Christ's suffering on our behalf, and so much more. During the writing process, the lyrics to an old hymn kept echoing through my mind. I thought we could conclude our week together by ruminating on the words.

### The Solid Rock

*My hope is built on nothing less*

*Than Jesus' blood and righteousness;*

*I dare not trust the sweetest frame,*

*But wholly lean on Jesus' name.*

*When darkness seems to hide His face,*

*I rest on His unchanging grace;*

*In every high and stormy gale,*

*My anchor holds within the veil.*

*His oath, His covenant, His blood*

*Support me in the whelming flood;*

*When all around my soul gives way,*

*He then is all my hope and stay.*

*When He shall come with trumpet sound,*

*Oh, may I then in Him be found;*

*Dressed in His righteousness alone,*

*Faultless to stand before the throne.*

*On Christ, the solid Rock, I stand;*

*All other ground is sinking sand,*

*All other ground is sinking sand.*[91]


Jesus Christ—My Lord—My Savior—My Hope and Stay

# WEEK 7
## Until He Comes
### 1 PETER 4:1-11

*So as to live the rest of the time in the flesh no longer*
*for the lusts of men, but for the will of God.*
1 Peter 4:2

*There is no course more safe or blessed than to live in the will of God.* [92]
~ F.B. Meyer

Christ became a man, putting on flesh that He might experience everything that we experience. Peter tells us, "Christ suffered in the flesh" (1 Peter 4:1). Consequently, we are to look to Christ and respond as He did. His attitude should be our attitude. We should desire to do the will of the Father instead of our own will, just as Jesus did.

But how do we accomplish this? So often, we try to live the Christian life through the power and energy of the flesh. This is an impossibility. It is only through the power of the Holy Spirit that anyone can obey the Word of God and live as Christ did.

F.B. Meyer states we must:

> Realize that as one with Christ you have, in the mind of God, died. Deliberately choose that death at once and for evermore as your portion and lot. Then look to the Holy Spirit to put the sentence of death into daily and hourly execution. And you will find that, though the flesh still lives, it will no longer govern you; but the Spirit of God will govern it through you, robbing it of power, and keeping it so utterly in subjection that you may be tempted to think that it is changed in nature. This, however, will be a mistake, for if the Spirit's power is relaxed for only an instant, the old fatal habits will re-assert themselves, and if persisted in will work with more than their former force. [93]

It is in living out Galatians 2:20, the crucified life, that we experience the resurrection power of new life in Christ. As Meyer explains, it is a daily dying. We desire to deal with our flesh once and for all, but if you are like me, you know your flesh is all too willing to rear its ugly head. I must remain alert and on guard against the temptations that would arouse my flesh. It is as I crucify these old desires that the Spirit of God takes over with power beyond my ability.

This life is exactly what Peter experienced. Prior to Pentecost, Peter denied Jesus three times. But after His resurrection, Christ restored Peter to fruitful service. Jesus commissioned him to tend His sheep, to care for them out of His love for Christ. We see the precious mercy of our Lord as He chose Peter on the day of Pentecost to "feed His sheep" the gospel message and see 3,000 saved.

I am so grateful that the Bible doesn't gloss over people's lives. I am encouraged by Peter's restoration, which gives me great hope! In fact, when I compare it to what the world has to offer, it is truly outrageous!

# WEEK 7 · DAY ONE
## 1 PETER 4:1-11

I have enjoyed reading through 1 Peter as we have prepared this study. One of the most meaningful practices I have employed is reading an individual portion of Scripture, slowly and out loud.

Read 1 Peter 4:1-11 out loud.

As you do, allow the Holy Spirit to nourish your inner man through the Word of God.

1a.  Now read 1 John 1:5-10. What is the message we have heard?

1b.  How should this message impact our lives?

Peter and John penned the same message. We are to live our lives "no longer for the lusts of men but for the will of God" (1 Peter 4:2). This change requires a difference in focus. We must direct our minds and hearts toward God. In fact, Dallas Willard says,

> And when we come to the task of developing disciples into the fullness of Christ, we must be very clear that one main part, and by far the most fundamental, is to form the insights and habits of the student's mind so that it stays directed toward God. When this is adequately done, a full heart of love will go out toward God, and joy and obedience will flood the life.[94]

2. Take a moment to reflect. In moments of leisure, to what does your mind automatically go?

3. How do you personally seek to live for God's will and not your own?

The Tyndale Commentary states, "For being put to death as He was, is the only form of 'suffering' that decisively brings a person's sinning to an end."[95] That is why we are to consider ourselves dead, "crucified with Christ" (Galatians 2:20).

4. Read Luke 9:23. How do you obey the command of Christ and acknowledge your death to sin on a daily basis?

Discipleship must include evangelism and the teaching of all that Christ commanded. Many in our churches have never been formally discipled. But it is the individual's responsibility to seek out more mature Christians and learn from their lives and their writings.

5. How have you sought to be a faithful disciple of Christ?

The following words of Dallas Willard serve as a challenge to me; may they challenge you as well.

> So, as Jesus' current assistant in His ongoing program, one important way of characterizing our work of 'training disciples to do everything told you' is 'bringing them to actually believe all the things they have already heard.' Our task in ourselves and in others is to transform right answers into automatic responses to real-life situations.[96]

6. Reflect on that last phrase: "to transform right answers into automatic responses to real-life situations." How do we go about this and how would doing so change our lives?

The early Christians associated themselves with the death of Christ and considered themselves cut off from the world. The fleshly indulgences of the world and many of the sins of their former lives had been forsaken. It was their "separateness" that caused the world to malign and persecute them. Realizing that their citizenship was in Heaven, they lived as pilgrims and sojourners on the earth. We would do well to follow their example.

Read 1 Peter 4:3-7.

Could it be that our affections for the world keep us from fully surrendering and following Christ? Why is it that many of the sins listed in this passage are also seen in the lives of some who profess Christ? This obviously should not be. But we are not just seeking behavior modification. We must change from the inside out. It is as our affections are diverted from the things of the world to Christ and His will that we are truly changed. Then God opens our eyes to things that are eternal and the things of earth do grow strangely dim.

We must say "no" to consumer Christianity and "yes" to a call of commitment to the perfect will of the Father.

1a.  Read Romans 6:11-13. What sin has held you captive making you a slave?

Is it worry, anxiety, unforgiveness, lust, immorality, jealousy, covetousness or greed? Sin is not to be master over us.

1b.  How do you deal with revealed sin?

2. Read James 1:13-15.  How does James describe temptation that leads to sin?

Nothing has power over me that I have not given power through my own desires or lust. Jesus was able to say that Satan had no part in Him (John 14:30). It is as we confess and forsake our sin that we are forgiven and cleansed. I must ask the Lord to show me the root of my sin. What need am I trying to fulfill in a sinful way? Thus my lust and idolatry are exposed that they may not be rationalized away (everybody is doing it) but taken to the cross.

Our life before Christ was spent fulfilling our own will and desires. There should be a difference in our lives "after" Christ.

3. How has your life changed and do you ever share that change as part of your testimony?

Those who are not Christians genuinely think it strange that we would not carouse with them and that we would uphold the Word of God as our standard of righteousness and life.

4. Have you ever been maligned or persecuted because of a stand for Christ and His Word?

5. Look at 1 Peter 4:6. What do you think is meant by "the gospel has been preached even to those who are dead"?

Most commentaries agree that the better translation would be "the gospel has been preached even to those who are *now* dead." Many among their ranks were being martyred. Peter is encouraging them to be faithful that they too might pass from this earthly struggle to "live in the Spirit according to the will of God" (1 Peter 4:6).

# WEEK 7 · DAY THREE
## 1 PETER 4:8

*Love is the comprehensive virtue that should complete and crown all other activity*
*(cf. Col. 3:14). It ought to be treated as the priority in Christian living.*[97]

Today we will focus on just one verse, 1 Peter 4:8. In our increasingly hostile and offended culture, we are to be a refreshing presence of grace and truth. It is possible to disagree on issues and still love those who espouse differing opinions. This is especially true on social media.

Be careful that you don't "pile on" a person who you don't know personally. So often all you know of the situation is what you have read on social media. I can tell you after being involved with those who have been misrepresented and having been misrepresented myself, the whole truth is very rarely presented.

Speak to issues; don't seek to assassinate another's character or intent. Remember what we just read. "Above all, love each other deeply, because love covers a multitude of sins" (1 Peter 4:8).

1.  How well do you represent Christ on social media?

2.  How have you seen the enemy hijack social media for divisive and slanderous means?

Be careful that you prayerfully respond on social media or in conversations. I have seen someone tweet or post something inappropriate only to quickly remove it. But the post was not removed before someone else took a screenshot and reposted it to their great humiliation. Posts are like spoken words; they can never be taken back.

3.  In our verse today, Peter states, "love covers". How can you practice covering with love?

Anxiety, depression and suicide rates have escalated rapidly in recent years. The Centers for Disease Control (CDC) recently released a report "suggesting that America's suicide rate increased by 25% between 1999 and 2016."[98]

Sadly, 12-17 year olds had a 63% increase in diagnosed depression from 2013-2016. What caused the increase? Dr. Laurel Williams, chief of psychiatry at Texas Children's Hospital observes, "Many people are worried about how busy they are. There's a lack of community. There's the amount of time that we spend in front of screens and not in front of other people. If you don't have a community to reach out to, then your hopelessness doesn't have any place to go."[99]

*Real love touches and gets involved in the messiness of life.*

Did you notice some of the causes that Dr. Williams points out? God created us for relationship. We are most satisfied and fulfilled when we are in right relationship with the Lord and with others. But we must spend time with others to be connected. It is nice to catch up with people's lives on social media by watching their children grow and viewing their life from afar. But a real relationship is not virtual – it is actual. We need time "with" others to deepen friendships and satisfy the longing in our souls.

After reading these statistics and watching the news about the opioid crisis, we know people are crying out to be seen and to be loved.

4.  How are you currently praying for and seeking to help someone in need?

Real love touches and gets involved in the messiness of life. We know that all people are created in the image of God and all of us need to be loved.

5. Make a list of some tangible ways you can love others. Think about those in your own home and family.

6. Now, make a list of how you can love your neighbor.

I have been reading a book recently, *The Justice Calling: Where Passion Meets Perseverance.* The authors state, "The two greatest commandments identified by Jesus – to love God and to love your neighbor as yourself – are the flip side of the two most prevalent sins throughout Scripture: idolatry and injustice. Failing to love God leads to idolatry, while failing to love others leads to injustice."[100]

7. How can you fight injustice by loving your neighbor?

Love is a verb. It will move us to action. It meets needs. I am always challenged when I treat 1 Corinthians 13:4-7 as a checklist to evaluate my current state of love. Real love forgives and believes the best; it never fails.

8. How would you rate on this love checklist?

Because God loves everyone and every person has been created in His image, we should love all people and grant them significance as image bearers of God. We should seek to love others in tangible ways. Sometimes it will be a sacrifice of time, money or convenience. Other times it will be an action that we might not think is significant and yet it might be just what that person needs at the moment – a word of encouragement, a smile, or a simple hug.

I received a gift of love recently. There was a family visiting Bellevue from Dallas, Texas. They came back to Guest Central to meet my husband and I after the first worship service. The father asked if he might pray for my husband. We all bowed our heads and as he was praying, his little daughter, Chloe, who was 6 years old, leaned over to me and wrapped both arms around my waist in the most precious and tender hug. I was so moved by her spontaneous affection, that I knelt beside her after we finished praying and asked to have my picture taken with her.

Children are so loving and innocent. Her sweet hug was like an expression of affection from the Lord. May we be ever conscious of those around us who might just need a gentle hug as an expression of acceptance and love.

The Christians who were the original recipients of Peter's letter were being scattered in the midst of persecution. Many were traveling as missionaries. Peter explains that it is incumbent upon believers to open their homes to each other and thus advance the gospel.

Read 1 Peter 4:9.

In their book, *The Simplest Way to Change the World,* the authors state, "Yes, all people need the local church; they also need a spiritual hospital in their neighborhood. They need someone who loves Jesus and lives near them to act out the gospel for them by welcoming them and exuding the warmth that only people who have already been helped and healed by Jesus can give."[101]

1.  How are you opening your home and offering love, safety, and gospel grace to your hurting neighbors?

Do you remember the difference between hospitality and entertaining? Entertaining puts the emphasis on what you have done to prepare for your guests, while hospitality puts the focus on your guests and how thrilled you are to have time with them. When people feel welcome and enjoyed, they could care less how you decorate your home or if you use paper plates or china.

2.  Read 1 Timothy 5:10; Hebrews 13:2; Romans 12:13 and 1 Timothy 3:2. Who do these verses address?

Hospitality is important and is a characteristic of Christ followers. Think about the life of Jesus. He did not own a home, yet He lived a life of hospitality. He was always inviting people to be with Him.

In her book, *The Gospel Comes with a House Key,* Rosaria Butterfield says, "Radically ordinary hospitality is this: using your Christian home in a daily way that seeks to make strangers neighbors, and neighbors family of God. It brings glory to God, serves others, and lives out the gospel in word and deed."[102] Do you think of hospitality as ordinary? Is it something that is relatively easy for you to do, or do you cringe at the thought of opening your home to others?

Because I grew up in a home that practiced radically ordinary hospitality, it is "ordinary" for me. Right now, we have a young couple living with us for a month before they move to a new location. I had my discipleship group over for lunch today and invited a sweet single mom that I met through ministering in the city to come and bring her children. We laughed and talked over a meal. We shared prayer concerns and paused to pray over one of the teens who was struggling. Operating in the grace and hospitality of the gospel should become our native tongue. But it will only happen as we die to self and embrace the call of our Father to love with abandon.

Do you still have children living in your home? Be the home that their friends enjoy coming to. I know it will cost you extra for additional groceries and probably less sleep, but the payoff far exceeds the investment.

3. What is one step you will take to begin to embrace radically ordinary hospitality?

4. What are some of your favorite ideas for hospitality? Be prepared to share them with your small group. A favorite recipe would be nice to share also!

Read 1 Peter 4:10-11.

We are gifted for the service and building up of the Church. We are also gifted to be a more accurate reflection of Christ to a lost world. Thus, our gifts are not for us, but always for the benefit of others.

5. What is your primary spiritual gift and how are you currently using it to bless the Body of Christ? (If you do not know your spiritual gift, go to www.bellevue.org/discovering-spiritualgifts and take the test.)

Read 1 Peter 4:1-11.

Verses 1-6 warn us to prepare for suffering and to be aware that there will be people who will not understand our "separate" life and will try to pressure us into returning to our old way of life. We no longer live for our old sinful desires but for the will of God.

But we must be on guard and stay alert. We have a very real enemy who schemes against us. We can never believe the lie that we have "arrived" or have it all together. We are completely dependent upon the Holy Spirit to fill and guide us. The Bible is clear that pride comes before a fall (Proverbs 16:18).

1.  Take a moment to ask the Lord to reveal any areas where the enemy is tempting you to compromise. Write down anything He reveals and then confess your sin that you might be cleansed (1 John 1:9).

We must follow the example of Christ, Who gave the devil no ground in His life.

Read 1 Peter 4:7-11.

2.  Make a list of the call to action for Christians in verses 7-11.

Read these verses again from the Message translation:

> Therefore, be earnest and disciplined in your prayers. Most important of sins. Cheerfully share your home with those who need a meal or a place to stay. God has given each of you a gift from his great variety of spiritual gifts. Use them well to serve one another. Whoever speaks, *is to do so* as one who is speaking the utterances of God; whoever serves *is to do so* as one who is serving by the strength which God supplies; so that in all things God may be glorified through Jesus Christ, to whom belongs the glory and dominion forever and ever. Amen.

*When we humble ourselves and live according to God's Word, He not only empowers us, but He also enables us to point others to Jesus as we bring glory to Him alone.*

We are to pray, love, share, serve, and glorify God. What a beautiful description of the life to which we have been called!

3.   Who empowers this supernatural living? (v. 11)

When we humble ourselves and live according to God's Word, He not only empowers us, but He also enables us to point others to Jesus as we bring glory to Him alone. We have studied other verses that explain how we are to live to glorify God.

4.   Read Colossians 3:17. Through what means are we to bring Him glory?

> *Do it with all the strength and energy that God supplies.*
> *Then everything you do will bring glory to God through Jesus Christ.*
> *All glory and power to him forever and ever! Amen.*
> 1 Peter 4:11b (NLT)

Amy Hannon bases her delightful cookbook, *Love, Welcome, Serve* on 1 Peter 4:8-11. She says we are to "Love deeply. Welcome gladly. Serve faithfully. So that in all things God may be praised."[103]

Amy calls Biblical hospitality, authentic and intentional. She says, "When you purposefully pour yourself into others, the treat will be yours, too! There's something unique and magical about serving. It'll come right back around and squeeze your heart."[104] We know that we will reap what we sow (Galatians 6:7).

5.  How are you sowing seeds of intentional hospitality for your family and neighbors?

As you obey the Lord to pray, love, share, serve, and glorify Him, you will find that you cannot keep it to yourself. You will want to share with others how the Lord is moving in your life, how He is opening doors of service and relationship and how you have been blessed in the midst. Making Him known is the mandate He has left for us (Matthew 28:19). As we open our homes, we must also open our lives and our mouths to share the gospel.

In fact, remember our verse in 1 Peter 3 about being ready to make a defense of our hope? "But sanctify Christ as Lord in your hearts, always *being* ready to make a defense to everyone who asks you to give an account for the hope that is in you, yet with gentleness and reverence" (1 Peter 3:15).

If you have sanctified Christ as Lord and are opening your life and home to others, you will be given opportunities to share the gospel. Seeing someone come to faith in Christ is the greatest joy and hope on this earth.

It all goes back to keeping the main thing, the main thing – Loving God and loving our neighbors!

As we close our study for the week, I wanted to share a couple of paragraphs from a blog post that our daughter recently wrote for Missional Motherhood. It sums up our calling and will be a great way to summarize our week's focus.

> Loving others and making disciples are at the core of Christianity. While I do plan to continue with those banana bread drop offs and meals, I also want the heart of everything I'm doing to be about the gospel. This is the greatest gift I have ever been given. The saving grace I've freely received compels me to offer that same gift to all as I'm given the opportunity. I open my home so my guests will know His heart. By sharing the gospel that defines me, I am sharing my life.

So, let's host dinner parties, small groups, overnight guests and potlucks. Let's open up our homes and lives to others, but let us never forget to also open our mouths and proclaim the saving grace of Jesus Christ our Lord.[105]

# WEEK 8
## When Life is Hard

### 1 PETER 4:12-19

*Beloved, do not be surprised at the fiery ordeal among you, which comes upon you for your testing, as though some strange thing were happening to you; but to the degree that you share the sufferings of Christ, keep on rejoicing, so that also at the revelation of His glory you may rejoice with exultation.*

1 Peter 4:12-13

*I believe there is no place where we learn so much, and have so much light cast upon Scripture, as we do in the furnace. Read a truth in hope, read it in peace, read it in prosperity, and you will not make anything of it. Be put inside the furnace (and nobody knows what a bright blaze is here who has not been there) and you will be then able to spell all hard words and understand more than you ever could without it.[106]*

~ Charles Spurgeon

Suffering is the theme for the portion of Scripture we will be studying this week. While none of us will ever experience the horrors the early church endured or even the terrible persecution many Christians are currently undergoing in many parts of the world, we can all benefit from learning to exhibit grace in the midst of suffering.

Peter uses the word "suffering" and its derivatives over 20 times in this short letter. The readers of his original letter were living in a time when extreme persecution against Christians was rapidly escalating. Hatred towards God and His people was reaching a fevered pitch. For instance, Emperor Nero was arresting Christians, covering them with tar, and setting them ablaze to light his garden parties. Peter surely felt constrained to reassure his readers of God's sovereign purposes and plans for His people despite appearances to the contrary.

Peter wants his readers to respond well when faced with suffering. A particular recollection of his own poor reaction in the midst of a crisis remained burned in his memory banks. As you will recall on the verge of the crucifixion, Jesus knowing Peter would deny Him three times, said, "Simon, Simon, behold, Satan has demanded permission to sift you like wheat; but I have prayed for you, that your faith may not fail; and you, when once you have turned again, strengthen your brothers" (Luke 22:31-32).

Peter's faith would falter in the course of the brutality of the arrest, trial, and crucifixion of Jesus, but his failure would not be final. In God's timing, Peter, full of the Holy Spirit, would preach and more than 3000 would come to know Jesus. Serving Jesus and suffering for the sake of the gospel would ultimately mark Peter as a choice vessel in the Kingdom of God. He is charged with the task of bolstering the courage of God's people in the face of affliction and persecution and he fulfills his calling. Who better to address the issue of suffering for the cause of Christ than Peter, one who has experienced both failure and success in this area.

# ⇒ WEEK 8 · DAY ONE ⇐

Read I Peter 4:12.

Peter opens the passage we will be studying this week with the rather soul-rattling pronouncement that enduring affliction for the cause of Christ is consistent with "the faith which was once for all handed down to the saints" (Jude 1:3b). Properly understood, sharing the sufferings of Christ is actually a reason for extraordinary joy because of the outrageous hope we have in Him!

Earlier in his letter, Peter writes, "In this you greatly rejoice, even though now for a little while, if necessary, you have been distressed by various trials, so that the proof of your faith, being more precious than gold which is perishable, even though tested by fire, may be found to result in praise and glory and honor at the revelation of Jesus Christ" (1 Peter 1:6-7).

With pastoral tenderness Peter addresses his audience as "beloved." Perhaps the insertion of this term was a reminder of God's love as well as his own for them. In times of affliction and persecution, believers can be tempted to doubt the lovingkindness of the Father.

"Peter's term for 'fiery ordeal' is a single Greek word, *pyrōsis*. It refers to an agonizing experience of burning with fire."[107] While we do not know the specifics, we can surmise the current suffering was directly related to their testimony for Christ. It is important to note that not every difficulty in life is necessarily a fiery trial caused by our relationship with Jesus. We live in a sin-cursed world, and some of the difficulties we face are simply a part of the human experience. It is equally important to understand that some trials come upon us as the direct result of our personal disobedience and sin. They are the consequences of sinful choices. God has given us a free will. We are free to choose to obey Christ or to indulge the flesh. However, we are not free to choose the consequences of our poor choices.

Learn this. Sin always causes suffering, but not all suffering is the result of sin. Peter is addressing a group of believers who are being afflicted for the cause of Christ. Evidently, their initial reaction to the escalating persecution is one of surprise, "as though some strange thing were happening" (1 Peter 4:12). Somewhere in our personal theology most (if not all of us) have garnered the mistaken notion that knowing Jesus insulates us from pain and persecution. Nothing could be further from the truth! The source of suffering can often be traced to our personal relationship with Jesus. We should not be surprised when God allows difficult circumstances to become our companion on our pilgrim's journey towards eternity with Christ.

The original recipients of Peter's letter were living in the Greco-Roman society. Their Christian belief system and their subsequent behavior was in marked contrast with the culture, putting them at odds with the community at large. Extreme persecution was the regrettable result.

Read Matthew 16:24-26.

Peter had heard Jesus caution His followers regarding suffering, which is often the result of fellowship and devotion.

1. What does this passage teach us about the cost of following Jesus?

If you are a Jesus-follower, you should not be surprised by the afflictions or "fiery ordeals" that befall you. Christ suffered at the hands of wicked men who despised Him and rejected His claim as the Messiah. Christ forewarned His followers, "You will be hated by all because of My name" (Matthew 10:22). He continued this line of thought, "A disciple is not above his teacher, nor a slave above his master. It is enough for the disciple that he become like his teacher, and a servant like his master. If they have called the head of the house Beelzebul, how much more will they malign the members of his household!" (Matthew 10:24-25).

Read John 15:18-21.

2a. How does Jesus describe our relationship with the world after our conversion?

2b. Why does the world hate us?

While Peter's imagery of a fiery furnace here portrays the painful experience of persecution, fire can also be used to purge impurities. Perhaps Peter had in mind a dual purpose for the fiery trials his readers were experiencing. Could he also be picturing the refining process of God, resulting in spiritual maturity?

God creatively uses a variety of methods to progressively change us into the image of Christ. When we are a willing participant in His process of sanctification, God is able to more quickly purge the sinful habit patterns of our flesh and move us along in our spiritual growth. If we stubbornly resist His refining process, we merely exacerbate God's course of action and force Him to repeat the procedure, many times if necessary.

God desires to "present to Himself the church in all her glory; having no spot or wrinkle or any such thing, but that she should be holy and blameless" (Ephesians 5:27). In order for this to happen, a whole lot of flesh must be purged out of the church and the individual members of it! God's most effective tool for purification is the refining fire of trials.

Read Isaiah 48:10.

3a. God uses the refining fires of trials and tests in order to grow our faith and crucify our flesh. What is one of the purposes of affliction?

3b. How has God used affliction in your life to burn away some of the dross?

3c. Ultimately, what did affliction produce in your experience?

Proverbs 17:3 says, "The refining pot is for silver and the furnace for gold, but the Lord tests hearts." If you are fully committed to becoming a woman after God's own heart, He will have to purify your heart in the refinery and burn away the dross of the flesh, leaving behind the gold of His glory and grace.

The New Testament version of this same idea is found in John 15:1-11. Read this passage.

4a. Who is the True Vine?

4b. Who is the Vinedresser?

4c. What is the job of the Vinedresser?

4d. Why?

4e. How does the gardener coax more fruit from the vines?

4f. How is the Father glorified?

God must prune and perfect His child in order to remove those things that inhibit or impair our spiritual growth. However, some pruning can be avoided if we will examine our lives in light of God's holy standard and make adjustments accordingly. We can choose to walk circumspectly and avoid His shears to some extent. However, "it is God who is at work in [us], both to will and to work for His good pleasure" (Philippians 2:13). God is doing what He deems to be necessary to conform us to the image of Jesus Christ. It is up to Him to decide how much refining is needed. It is up to us to exhibit grace in the midst of it.

Peter's goal as he prepares to draw his letter to a conclusion seems to be to encourage his readers, reminding them of the goodness and sovereignty of God, especially in difficult times. Could any portion of Scripture be more poignant to us as we attempt to navigate the minefield of a culture set against God and His Son? Oh, that we might fix our eyes on Jesus and take courage while we experience the outrageous hope and extravagant joy He alone provides!

Joy is the birthright of every believer. Psalm 16:11b says, "In Your presence is fullness of joy." Joy is available to all believers, but the attainment of it is not automatic. The joy of the Lord must be individually appropriated. If the presence of joy were standard equipment for all believers, Paul would not command us to engage in its pursuit. In Philippians 3:1a the apostle writes, "Rejoice in the Lord." Joy is the by-product of practicing the presence of Jesus.

Jesus offers us unlimited supply of His joy. In fact, "His divine power has granted to us everything pertaining to life and godliness, through the true knowledge of Him who called us by His own glory and excellence" (2 Peter 1:3). Joy is just one of the bequests our salvation ensures.

I wrote this closing illustration in 2007. The incident occurred in our former house; the application is timeless.

> God reminds me of the fullness of joy available to me through Jesus Christ. Our home was built 15 years ago. Time is taking a toll on our house. Several weeks ago, on a Sunday morning, we were getting ready to attend our Bible Study Fellowship and church service. Standing in our master bathroom, I heard running water. After several moments, I located the source of the leak. Water was coming from a cracked plumbing joint in our closet. Panicked, I called for my husband. In one motion, he shut off the water valve and pulled up the wet carpet. He set up several fans in hope of salvaging the carpet. Surviving the wet mess, we both decided to continue with our plans and go to church. In light of what had just happened, we felt we needed to be at church! We managed to get to church in time for the sermon and picked up some plumbing supplies on the way home. Once home, my husband immediately set about trying to repair the leak. Fortunately, the fix was not difficult. Satisfied the repair was secure, we both sat down in the den. Only then did we discover the water had run under the wall from the closet to the den. Nearly one-third of the den carpet was soaked. Furniture was moved. Wet carpet was pulled up. More fans were set out. Early in the morning, I had consciously determined not to lose my joy over the big wet mess in my house. I reaffirmed my heart's desire to the Lord. I would not cave to my frustration. After what Jesus had done for me on the cross, I determined to stay in His presence and choose joy! [108]

The story I concluded with yesterday has more to it. Let me continue to share:

On the following Saturday I was getting ready to attend a baby shower for my daughter-in-law. Obviously excited over the event, I was preoccupied with anticipation. I was standing in front of my vanity applying my makeup when I suddenly realized the carpet was wet. Again, I called for my husband. I am known for drama, but the high pitch of my voice revealed my panic. 'The carpet is wet,' I squealed. 'Again? Are you serious?' he replied in genuine shock. Further investigation revealed a leak in the plumbing behind the shower stall. The leak required the shower stall to be removed along with the vanity and mirror. Drywall and insulation had to be removed to the studs. The closets were emptied. The bathroom was gutted. The carpet was ruined. Walls were removed. Wallpaper was damaged. Light fixtures were removed. Again, I was faced with a decision. Would I lose my joy in this plumbing journey? I am happy to report my joy remained intact. After what Jesus did for me on the cross, I determined the loss of some wood, hay, and stubble was of little consequence. I appropriate His joy by faith. I rise above the downward pull of the world, the flesh, and the devil. I fix my mind on Jesus. I run to my strong tower. I choose joy!

For several weeks, we lived in chaos. The contents of our closets were stacked in our bedroom. Shoe racks lined the walls. Occasionally, I was forced to do the mental gymnastics necessary to cast down vain imaginations, but I survived the test with my joy intact.

Little did I know my joy quotient would be tested yet again. Just three weeks after the shower leak, my clothes washer would not cycle through the final rinse. Mounds of billowy soap bubbles clung to the clothes, requiring multiple washings. The cable server went out. Our Internet access was lost. In the scheme of things, these are small annoyances. Learn this truth. Minor irritations can be joy-robbers. We tend to gear up for the big events in life, but the little frustrations can grate on our nerves, leaving us prickly and bad-tempered. Solomon says, 'Catch the foxes for us, the little foxes that are ruining the vineyards, while our vineyards are in blossom' (Song of Solomon 2:15). The little aggravations can sneak in and steal our joy.

That evening we went to bed joking, 'What else can happen?' Around 1:00 a.m. that question was answered. We were startled awake by the sound of ripping drywall. The ceiling in our master bedroom collapsed! Our upstairs water-heater sprang a leak and dumped 50 gallons of water and wet insulation in our bedroom. Thankfully, the bulk of the ceiling landed on our armoire and not on our heads. Water sheeted down the front of the armoire and the television housed in the cabinet. The sound of the collapse was frightening; the sight was staggering. My husband turned off the water and then ran upstairs. When he returned to our bedroom, I was sitting upright in the bed with the covers clutched to my throat. My mouth was still open. My eyes were riveted to the hole in our ceiling and the wet piles of pink insulation.

When I could pull myself from my perch, I discovered splatters of wet insulation had settled in my shoes, spotted my sweaters, and soaked stacks of our clothes still awaiting closet repairs before they could be stored. The carpet was steadily soaking up water like a dry sponge. The oriental rug under my bed appeared to be ruined. The dyes on the once-beautiful rug were bleeding together and forming puddles of mottled colors. I stood in the doorway of my bedroom and surveyed the scene. A decision was required. Would I experience joy in the journey or would I sell out eternal reward for earthy remnants? Would I maintain my spiritual equilibrium or fall in the pit of despair? The choice was mine to make. I chose joy!

After what Jesus has done on my behalf, I have no right to lose my joy. The manifestation of the joy of Jesus, especially in the midst of difficult circumstances, validates the presence and power of Christ in the believer.[109]

*Unspeakable joy. Unshakeable joy. Undeniable joy. Unparalleled joy. In the midst of our any and every circumstance, joy. Through the ups and downs and the twists and turns of life, joy. In His presence there is fullness of joy.*

Beloved, Jesus bequeathed His joy on us as part and parcel of our conversion. Jesus said, "These things I have spoken to you so that My joy may be in you, and that your joy may be made full" (John 15:11). Unspeakable joy. Unshakeable joy. Undeniable joy. Unparalleled joy. In the midst of our any and every circumstance, joy. Through the ups and downs and the twists and turns of life, joy. In His presence there is fullness of joy.

Read I Peter 4:13.

We gladly receive His gift of joy and eagerly embrace it, but let's place the joy of the Lord in the context of suffering. The recipients of Peter's letter were suffering unimaginable hardship, but he urged them to "rejoice with exultation" for the privilege of sharing in "the sufferings of Christ." Suffer with joy? This is weighty stuff. Enduring trials is one thing; exulting in them is quite another! Only God can give us sustainable joy in the midst of difficult circumstances. We do not rejoice in the trial itself. We rejoice in the fresh vision of the peace and presence of God in the midst of our trouble and in the spiritual maturity being produced in us, as we not only endure, but also exult in the sufferings of Christ.

Look up Matthew 5:10-12.

In this passage, Jesus teaches the proper response to insults and persecution for the cause of Christ.

1a.  What instruction does He give?

1b.  Why?

Joy far exceeds the emotion of happiness. Unbelievers will experience isolated moments of happiness; believers have the joy of Jesus Christ continually available through the indwelling Spirit of the Living God abiding in them.

Read James 1:2-4.

2a.  According to this passage what is a Christian's response to be in the midst of various trials?

2b.  Why?

2c.  What is the end result of endurance?

James is not glibly suggesting that you and I enjoy sorrow and suffering. Rather he is establishing the supernatural reality that when (not if) trials and tests intrude upon the believer's life, God has a purpose in mind.

Take heart, "knowing that the testing of your faith produces endurance. And let endurance have its perfect result, that you may be perfect and complete, lacking in nothing." Take joy in the fact that, for the Christian, suffering has a purpose. It is not a random condition or inadvertent situation that has befallen you. It is a divinely orchestrated circumstance and season designed to produce endurance because when endurance has its perfect result, the emerging child of God is both "perfect and complete, lacking in nothing" (James 1:4b). And that is a reason to have joy, beloved!

Peter's letter echoes the same thought in 1 Peter 4:13. The response of joy in the midst of unjust suffering seems unthinkable. Yet, the response of joy to cruelty and hardship is what dramatically sets us apart from those outside a personal relationship with Christ.

Read Philippians 1:27-30.

3a.  Regardless of our circumstances, how should we live?

3b.  According to Philippians 1:29 what has God granted to us?

Responding with joy and exultation to persecution and pain is completely unacceptable to the natural man. Yet, God's Word instructs us, and God's Spirit enables us to react with joy, giving undeniable validation of our genuine conversion experience.

As John MacArthur explains, "God not only gave believers the marvelous gift of faith to believe in Him, but also the privilege to suffer for His sake." [110] God has given us faith to believe and grace to behave! "For I consider that the sufferings of this present time are not worthy to be compared with the glory that is to be revealed to us" (Romans 8:18).

Rejoice in the midst of suffering and "keep on rejoicing, so that also at the revelation of His glory you may rejoice with exultation" (1 Peter 4:13b). Peter points to the coming of Christ as the paramount reason for joy. In 2 Corinthians 4:17-18 Paul writes, "For momentary, light affliction is producing for us an eternal weight of glory far beyond all comparison, while we look not at the things which are seen, but at the things which are not seen; for the things which are seen are temporal, but the things which are not seen are eternal." Keeping our eyes on Jesus, setting our minds on things above, living with a view of eternity will produce in us outrageous hope and extraordinary joy regardless of the circumstances!

The contemporary cultural philosophy views suffering as unpredictable and unavoidable, an innate consequence of the human condition. To the natural man, when crisis occurs, endurance, perhaps aided with self-medication, is the only option. Shortening the duration and minimizing the effects of suffering become the end game.

Contrary to our culture, we are considering suffering from a Biblical viewpoint. As believers, living counter-culturally, we are all vulnerable to the world's abhorrence and subsequent avoidance of difficult circumstances, but we must categorically refuse such thinking. Peter wants his readers to understand that suffering is often a part of God's divine purpose He has ordained for us. As much as we like to believe that being in the center of God's will protects us from any harm, that is not biblical. In reality, the center of God's will is often the source of our suffering! However painful this truth is to receive, we can trust in the sovereign purpose of God and rest in His tender mercies. Peter's letter offers outrageous hope and extraordinary joy for those in the midst of difficult circumstances. "Keep on rejoicing, so that also at the revelation of His glory you may rejoice with exultation" (1 Peter 4:13b). An attitude of exultation fuels our endurance when Christ is the object of our adulation.

Read 1 Peter 4:14.

Peter wants his readers to understand the spiritual value of suffering for the cause of Christ. In God's economy, suffering equals blessedness. That seems like a paradox, but who better than Peter to teach us such a seemingly contradictory truth?

Read about Peter's arrest and imprisonment in Acts 12:1-16.

1a.  After Peter's arrest what was the church doing?

1b. On the night when Peter was about to be brought before Herod and presumably put to death, what was Peter doing?

1c. God dispatched "an angel of the Lord." What happened when the angel arrived?

1d. Where did Peter go after he walked out of the prison?

1e. Mary opened the door and ran to announce Peter's arrival. What was the reaction of the prayer warriors?

Peter has been ordained by the Lord to strengthen the brethren in the midst of trials and tribulations. He also has firsthand experience with suffering for the cause of Christ. His instruction to us is both valid and valuable on many levels.

Peter reminds his readers that it is "the name of Christ" which is the source of hatred directed towards believers. His name is synonymous with who He is and what He represents both for those who receive Him and for those who reject Him. On a mission trip in Asia we were riding in a cab to the conference center where we would be teaching. Our driver, who appeared to be unable to speak English, had been given the address by a hotel employee. The plastic idol attached to the dashboard bore silent witness to our driver's allegiance to a false god. As we engaged in sharing our God stories among ourselves, I couldn't help but notice that our driver turned the volume up on his radio every time we mentioned the name of Jesus. While he obviously was not fluent in our language, he understood enough English to despise the name of Jesus and attempt to drown it out, at least in his vehicle!

"If you are reviled for the name of Christ, you are blessed because the Spirit of glory and of God rests on you" (1 Peter 4:14). Lest some confusion arises, be reminded that the Spirit of God permanently indwells every believer. However, when God's people suffer for the cause of Christ, a unique manifestation of God's glory rests on us.

Read Acts 6:8-15 and Acts 7:54-60.

2a.  Stephen is a mighty man of faith. How is Stephen described in Acts 6:8?

2b.  Ungodly men stirred up the people and Stephen was dragged before the Council. How is Stephen's face described in Acts 6:15?

This is an example of what Peter is writing to us about in the passage we are studying.

Now look at Acts 7:54-60. Stephen's defense infuriated the crowd and they were cut to the quick.

3.  According to Acts 6:55-56, Stephen "full of the Holy Spirit" looked into Heaven. What does he see?

After the ascension Jesus was "seated at the right hand of God" (Colossians 3:1; Psalm 110:1; Luke 22:69; and Ephesians 1:20).

4.  What can we learn about what the Lord does when a believer prepares to go into the presence of the Lord in Glory? I love this insight!

The mob began to stone Stephen, laying aside their robes at the feet of Saul. This is where we are first introduced to Saul of Tarsus who would later become the apostle Paul after a dramatic conversion experience on the street called Straight (see Acts 9:1-19).

5.  What is Stephen's parting prayer for his tormentors?

When God's people endure suffering for the cause of Christ, God's glory is manifested and His perfect attributes are set on display. We see God's glory resting on Peter when he was imprisoned for the cause of Christ. We see God's glory illuminating Stephen's face and accompanying his martyr's death. When we not only endure trials but exult in them, God's glory is declared and displayed.

During seasons of suffering "the Spirit of glory and of God rests on you." The Holy Spirit, in permanent residence in believers, gives rest and supernatural relief in the midst of suffering. Peter's choice of words conjures up the Old Testament imagery of God's presence resting on Mount Sinai (see Exodus 24:16-17; 34:5-8) and hovering over the tabernacle (see Exodus 40:34-38) and later the temple (see 1 Kings 8:11). As the brilliant cloud of "the glory of the Lord" rested in the tabernacle and the temple, so the Holy Spirit lives in and ministers to us today. Particularly during times of tribulation and seasons of suffering, the Spirit of God gives relief and refreshment as well as patience to endure and grace to exult.

When properly understood, trials, especially persecutions, lead us to deeper fellowship with Christ, to deeper anticipation of His coming, and to a deeper experience of His Spirit resulting in outrageous hope and extraordinary joy in Jesus!

When we not only endure trials but exult in them, God's *glory* is *declared* and displayed.

Peter has previously been addressing suffering in the context of Spirit-filled Christian living, not as the result of sin. Now he inserts a warning to believers.

Read 1 Peter 4:15-16.

Caution against such serious crimes seem out of place, considering the caliber of Christians Peter was addressing. Matthew Henry writes, "The best of men need to be warned against the worst of sins."[111] Peter seems to be metaphorically referring to the whole scope of sinful behavior, from the greater to the lesser, from murder to meddling. It is possible the enemies of God were alleging these types of accusations against believers in an effort to bring further unfair treatment on them.

The surprising inclusion of "a troublesome meddler" in a reference including criminal activities seems incompatible. Perhaps Peter singles out meddling because his readers may not have recognized the serious ramifications of such behavior. Perhaps meddling did not seem overtly sinful or inappropriate to them. However, interfering in the lives of others disrupts the peace and harmony of the local church and surrounding community.

Look up 1 Thessalonians 4:11-12.

1. What lifestyle should accompany our Christian conversion?

Beloved, as much as it is up to you, live a quiet life. Mind your own business. Work hard. Behave properly, especially towards unbelievers, in order that the testimony of Christ might not be damaged.

Read 2 Thessalonians 3:11-12.

2a.  What behavior does Paul instruct his readers to avoid?

2b.  What lifestyle is recommended?

If you suffer for living for Jesus, do not be ashamed if the culture, including your immediate or extended family, rejects or reviles you.

A reminder of the culture of Peter's day might help us put this in context. The Cult of Caesar was the state religion of the Roman empire. The reigning emperor was worshipped as a god, blending both political allegiance with religious duty. This style of rule helped emulsify the vast Roman Empire which was populated with multiple ethnic groups and myriads of religious practices. With the growing advent of Christianity, both the political and religious system was being challenged by their unshakable faith in the one true God of Abraham, Isaac, and Jacob, and His Son, Jesus Christ the Messiah.

Kenneth Wuest notes, "Christianity appeared as a rival claimant to world worship and dominion. The Lord Jesus, the Messiah of Israel, was looked upon in the Christian Church as the One who would someday come back and take the government of the world upon His shoulder."[112]

Their recognition of Jesus as Lord was not merely politically incorrect, it was considered by some to be high treason. This caused the government, as well as the masses, to look on Christians with suspicion, creating a hostile environment and feeding an escalating persecution bordering on genocide. Peter is instructing his readers to live in such a way that the only offense they can be found guilty of is living for Jesus.

Read Romans 12:9-18.

3a. According to this passage, what specific behaviors should characterize our lifestyle?

3b. Paul sums up the list in Romans 12:18. What does this verse say?

A similar admonition to live at peace with all men is recorded by the writer of Hebrews. "Pursue peace with all men, and the sanctification without which no one will see the Lord" (Hebrews 12:14). If it is possible, without denying Christ, pursue peace. Paul writes, "I urge that entreaties and prayers, petitions and thanksgivings, be made on behalf of all men, for kings and all who are in authority, so that we may lead a tranquil and quiet life in all godliness and dignity" (1 Timothy 2:1-2). We will not escape this life without a measure of hurt, heartache, and seasons of suffering. But God has given us supernatural strength to endure and grace to rejoice.

My youngest son was married on May 14, 2005, to the love of his life. As the big day approached, my mixed emotions, coupled with my rampant hormones, threatened to be my undoing. An odd mixture of unrestrained joy and profound sadness tugged at my mother's heart and sent me reeling from the vast extremes of my spectrum of emotions. At any moment I felt the dam that was precariously holding my feelings in check was in danger of bursting and flooding me with my pent-up emotions and carefully constrained tears.

On the day of the wedding I began to dress for the big event with a sense of growing excitement and mounting dread! Perhaps only another mother could unravel or understand the multitude of contradictory feelings that pulled unrelentingly at my mother's heart. My darling son, my baby, my youngest was about to take a bride. When our oldest son married, I felt as if a chapter of my life had turned over. On the eve of my youngest son marrying, I felt as if the whole book of mothering had been closed!

I began to dress long before my husband put on his tuxedo to go to the church. I did not want to feel rushed, and I was desperately trying to sort out my feelings before we arrived at the church for pictures. Knowing that seeing his bride for the first time in her wedding gown and veil would most likely precipitate a melt-down, I was attempting to steel myself against the raging tide of tears.

When our oldest son married in 2003, my husband surprised me at the rehearsal dinner with a pair of pearl earrings to wear at the wedding. When we had married, nearly thirty-one years before, he had given me a strand of pearls the night before our wedding. That string of pearls would be part of my mother-of-the-groom ensemble, and I was extremely touched by his very sentimental gift to me. As I prepared to leave for our youngest son's wedding, I stood in front of my bathroom mirror, fingering those pearl earrings and enjoying the memory of my husband's tender love gift. Dressed and ready to head to the church, I paused before putting my pearl studs in and reflected on their significance. Lost deep in thought, I was suddenly jarred back into reality as I watched in horror as the pearl earring slipped from my grasp and dropped down the drain of my bathroom sink!

Once again I was reminded that life is a series of crises, loosely strung together with occasional respites of peace! Some events are major crises and some fall into the minor category, but suffice it to say, life is a chaotic journey punctuated by moments of sheer madness! Peter's readership was suffering trials and tribulations. Some were minor while some were life-threatening. I have learned this about trials. Regardless of the depth and breadth of the test, if it is happening to you and your family, it is huge! Frankly, dropping my pearl earring down the drain on my son's wedding day was big...at least it was to me! Obviously in the big scheme of things, this was not the end of the world. But to me, on my son's wedding day, this was huge.

> The *glory* of the Christian life is not the absence of trials and tribulations. Rather, it is the *presence* of *Christ* in the midst of the crisis.

Even in my befuddled state of unbridled joy mingled with melancholy, I recognized the potential for disaster if I should choose to respond wrongly to this situation. As the mother of the groom, it mattered very little what earrings I wore and to sacrifice the day on the altar of such trivia would have been foolish and shameful. This minor disappointment was of little significance in light of the glorious event that was about to take place in my son's life as he and his bride pledged their lives and love to one another.

With that in mind, I grabbed a pair of pale purple drops that matched my dress, whispered a prayer of thanksgiving and sashayed out to the den. "Are you done already?" My husband asked in surprise. "Yes, I am, but I had a little mishap. I dropped my pearl earring down the drain, but not to worry, I will wear a different pair, and we can get it out of the drain later." Since things like this happen to me all the time, my husband did not bat an eye. He simply went to his tool chest and assured me he would have my earring out in no time. Despite my protests, he quickly removed the drain pipe and retrieved my earring out of the trap. Crisis solved!

Crises, big and small, are the natural outcome of living in a world that is cursed by sin. Such is the tool of God to hone off the rough edges of our lives and recreate us into the image of Christ. Through the process of trials, God is developing "the hidden person of the heart, with the imperishable quality of a gentle and quiet spirit, which is precious in the sight of God" (1 Peter 3:4). The glory of the Christian life is not the absence of trials and tribulations. Rather, it is the presence of Christ in the midst of the crisis. Therein lies the secret to our outrageous hope in Christ and the source of our extraordinary joy!

Peter continues to address suffering in the lives of believers, but he gives another reason for the cause of it. Suffering can be chastisement in order to purify the family of God.

Read 1 Peter 4:17-19.

The "household of God" seems to be a reference to the imagery of believers "as living stones . . . being built up as a spiritual house" (1 Peter 2:5a) for the Lord. Peter boldly declares, "It is time for judgement to begin with the household of God." Coming under the judgement of God seems to be a strange concept for us who have been forgiven in Christ. Paul describes believers this way, "You turned to God from idols to serve a living and true God, and to wait for His Son from Heaven, whom He raised from the dead, that is Jesus, who rescues us from the wrath to come" (1 Thessalonians 1:9-10). Make no mistake, beloved. Our sin debt has been paid in full by the shed blood of Jesus Christ and now we are no longer under the condemnation and judgement of God.

Look up Romans 8:1.

1. What does Paul teach us about our standing in Christ Jesus?

Before we leave this glorious truth concerning our salvation, may I remind you of the added blessings of our forgiveness. Not only has our sin been forgiven, but our guilt has also been removed. Psalm 32:5 says, "I acknowledged my sin to You, and my iniquity I did not hide; I said, 'I will confess my transgressions to the Lord'; and **You forgave the guilt of my sin**" (emphasis mine). Free from sin. Free from the guilt. Hallelujah! What a Savior!

Suffering may come through the avenue of persecution for the cause of Christ. Here, Peter is referring to God's chastisement due to sin in His children's lives and not the judgement leading to eternal condemnation, reserved for those who reject Jesus.

Read 1 Corinthians 11:31-32.

2a. How can we avoid coming under the corrective judgement of God?

2b. What can we expect from God if we do not include self-discipline in our devotional love for Him?

God disciplines His children. Hebrews 12:10-11 says, "He disciplines us for our good, so that we may share His holiness. All discipline for the moment seems not to be joyful, but sorrowful; yet to those who have been trained by it, afterwards it yields the peaceful fruit of righteousness." God chastens His own household, both individually and corporately. So, "what will be the outcome of those who do not obey the gospel of God?" This is undoubtedly a reference to eternal damnation in hell. It is far better to endure temporary suffering as believers because of purification or persecution than to bear eternal torment in the lake of fire (see Revelation 20:11-15).

Read the story of the rich man and Lazarus in Luke 16:19-31.

3a. How does Luke describe both men?

3b. At death, where does each man go?

It is worth noting that Jesus shares this story prior to His ascension to Heaven. Now, at the death of a believer, he/she is ushered immediately into the presence of the Lord in Glory.

3c.  Describe the conversation between the rich man and Father Abraham.

3d.  The rich man pleaded with Abraham to send someone to share salvation with his brothers and warn them of the judgement to come. What is Abraham's response?

The decision to repent of your sin, believe on the finished work of the Lord Jesus Christ, and receive Him by faith must be made prior to death. Hebrews 9:27 says, "It is appointed for men to die once and after this comes judgement." The promise of Heaven awaits the child of God; the promise of hell awaits "the godless man and the sinner" (1 Peter 4:18).

Suffering will come to everyone. Believers are not exempt from unjust suffering in the form of persecution, divine discipline, or for the purpose of purging. What sets apart suffering in the lives of God's people is that it is not without purpose. And that is the source of our rejoicing. We can entrust our souls "to a faithful Creator" and continue to do what is right and live fully in the outrageous hope and extraordinary joy of knowing Jesus.

# ☼ WEEK 9 ☼

## While We Wait

### 1 PETER 5:1-14

*After you have suffered for a little while, the God of all grace, who called you to*
*His eternal glory in Christ, will Himself perfect, confirm, strengthen and establish you.*
*To Him be dominion forever and ever. Amen.*
1 Peter 5:10-11

*One of the main teachings of the Bible is that almost no one grows into greatness or*
*finds God without suffering, without pain coming into our lives like smelling salts to wake*
*us up to all sorts of facts about life and our own hearts to which we were blind. For*
*reasons past our finding out, even Christ did not bring salvation and grace to us apart*
*from infinite suffering on the cross. As He loved us enough to face the suffering with*
*patience and courage, so we must learn to trust in Him enough to do the same. And as*
*His weakness and suffering, thus faced, led to resurrection power, so can ours.*[113]
~Tim Keller

Few people write letters any more. In fact, the U.S. Postal Service says the average American home receives only one personal letter about every two months. But, it really was not that long ago when the primary form of communication was a well thought out letter written with skillful penmanship. Today, text messaging and email trump what has become the lost art of letter writing. But think back for a minute to those days when letters were not only anticipated, they were valued and preserved.

When someone would write a letter, he or she would lead with the most important topics or news. Then as the end of the page came into view, a few last minute thoughts would be added in, often in smaller letters and perhaps even up the side of the sheet to cram more information onto the page.

Something similar is happening as we have reached the last part of Peter's epistle. He has completed the crux of his message to those scattered, first-century believers who were undergoing persecution and struggling to live out their faith. In I Peter 5, the old fisherman wraps up his letter with a few brief comments. And although these words were originally addressed to believers who had been driven out of Jerusalem and were dispersed all across Asia Minor, the message is relevant for all who are waiting with hope for the Kingdom of Christ.

Read 1 Peter 5:1-4.

Times of persecution require that God's people have the right people in leadership. Peter begins this passage with a message to the elders, God's appointed leaders in the church. The first mention of elders in the New Testament is in Acts 11:30 where Luke identifies them as the leaders of the church in Jerusalem. The New Testament uses three terms interchangeably to refer to these leaders: elder, bishop, and pastor. And they had one job—to shepherd the flock of God.

1.  In his address to these spiritual leaders, Peter first introduces himself. What three credentials does he give? (v.1)

    •

    •

    •

Throughout church history, the striking mark of a flourishing church is godly, mature, faithful leadership. Peter acknowledges these criteria and calls upon these leaders to be men of God because he knew if the leadership was not strong during this time of persecution, the church would fall apart.

2.  What command does Peter give to them at the beginning of verse 2?

The emphasis in verse 2 on the Shepherd and the sheep correlates with the parable Jesus tells in John 10 and the admonition He gave to Peter in John 21:15-17.

Read John 10:1-17.

3a.  What does Jesus call Himself in this parable?

3b.  Make note of the different ways Jesus says the Shepherd cares for His sheep.

Phillip Keller observes, "It is no accident that God has chosen to call us sheep. The behavior of sheep and human beings is similar in many ways…Sheep do not 'just take care of themselves' as some might suppose. They require, more than any other class of livestock, endless attention and meticulous care."[114]

Read John 21:15-17.

4.  Peter writes out of his own experiences with Jesus. What work does Jesus instruct Peter to do in these verses?

What shepherds are to sheep, elders/bishops/pastors are to the church body. Whatever the flock needs, the shepherd is to supply. Sheep must be led and they must be fed. When they are hurt, their wounds need to be bound; when they are in danger, they need to be rescued. When they stray away, they must be brought back into the fold. A good shepherd is always on the alert for and ready to defend his flock from enemies that prey upon them, even at the cost of personal sacrifice.

5.  What are the three warnings Peter mentions to these church leaders in 1 Peter 5:2-3?

In contrast to these negative elements, Peter challenges them to lead voluntarily and with eagerness, setting a good example for the flock. Charles Swindoll writes about this attitude of eagerness:

> There is nothing quite as exciting or delightful as a shepherd who emits enthusiasm. Such zeal is *contagious*! His love for the Scriptures becomes the flock's love for the Scriptures. His zest for life becomes the congregation's zest for life...His joyful commitment to obeying God becomes theirs...His passion for the unsaved becomes their passion.[115]

When leaders exude this exemplary kind of attitude, it inspires and motivates their flock, even in times of adversity.

6.  What hope does Peter give to these leaders in verse 4?

A number of crowns believers will receive are mentioned in the New Testament:

| CROWN | REFERENCE | RECIPIENTS |
|---|---|---|
| The Incorruptible Crown | 1 Corinthians 9:24-25 | Those who faithfully run the race |
| The Crown of Rejoicing | 1 Thessalonians 2:19 | Those who lead others to Christ |
| The Crown of Life | James 1:12 | Those who suffer tribulation and/or death for Christ |
| The Crown of Righteousness | 2 Timothy 4:8 | Those who live righteous lives |
| The Crown of Glory | 1 Peter 5:1-4 | Those who have led the flock of God faithfully |

The crown pictures the victor's crown that was given to winners in the Greek and Roman athletic games. Sometimes it would be made of laurel, sometimes myrtle, sometimes roses or oak leaves. Regardless of the composition, the leaves and flowers would soon fade away and the triumph would be forgotten. So it is with the things of this earth. But not so for believers who receive a crown—it will be an everlasting and unchanging reward. And what an unimaginable joy it will be for believers to one day place their crowns at the Savior's feet to "whom belongs the glory and dominion forever and ever" (1 Peter 4:11).

As you have read these verses today, you may be asking, "How does this apply to me?" We all have people in our lives who God has given us to lead. In other words, we all have a flock. Are you a mother? Tend your lambs. Do you supervise or influence people in the workplace? Do you have a leadership role at church? Feed His sheep. Are you a friend or a disciple maker? Tend His sheep.

7. Make a list of some practical ways you can tend to your flock.

*I urge you then to see that your 'flock of God' is properly fed and cared for. Accept the responsibility of looking after them willingly and not because you feel you can't get out of it, doing your work not for what you can make, but because you are really concerned for their well-being. You should aim not at being "little tin gods" but as examples of Christian living in the eyes of the flock committed to your charge.*

1 Peter 5:2-3 (PHILLIPS)

Throughout 1 Peter, the apostle has continually called for a posture of the heart, a way of life, that doesn't make sense to the world, goes against our flesh, yet is applauded by God and will be rewarded in Heaven. John Piper notes that, "Peter calls us again and again to think and feel and act in a way that can only be explained by an unshakeable, all-satisfying hope beyond this life."[116] So it is again with the verses we are focusing on today.

Read 1 Peter 5:5-7.

The main point of these verses is that believers are to be humble. Rarely does humility receive secular acclaim. In fact, humility is something that society really does not understand. An editorial in the September 12, 1994 edition of the Minneapolis Star Tribune summarized the reason American society has become hostile toward humility:

> There are some who naïvely cling to the nostalgic memory of God. The average churchgoer takes a few hours out of the week to experience the sacred . . But the rest of the time, he is immersed in a society that no longer acknowledges God as an omniscient and omnipotent force to be loved and worshiped. . .Today we are too sophisticated for God. We can stand on our own; we are prepared and ready to choose and define our own existence.[117]

When mankind thinks it can stand on its own, when we believe that we have evolved to a place where we are too "sophisticated" for God, humility dissipates because it will only thrive in the presence of God. And in the vacuum that occurs, the opposite of humility, pride, moves in.

1.  What traits do you associate with humility?

*Humility is perfect quietness of heart. It is for me to have no trouble; never to be fretted or vexed or irritated or sore or disappointed. It is to expect nothing, to wonder at nothing that is done to me, to feel nothing done against me. It is to be at rest when nobody praises me and when I am blamed or despised. It is to have a blessed home in the Lord where I can go in and shut the door and kneel to my Father in secret and be at peace as in a deep sea of calmness when all around is trouble. It is the fruit of the Lord Jesus Christ's redemptive work on Calvary's cross, manifested in those of His own who are definitely subject to the Holy Spirit.[118]*

~ Andrew Murray


*Humility is not thinking less of yourself, it's thinking of yourself less.[119]*

~ Rick Warren


2.   What characteristics do you associate with pride?




Humility and pride are both postures of the heart that color the way we view others. In the early 19th century, Thomas Carlyle wrote, "Every man is my superior in that I may learn from him."[120] That is a posture of humility. If we would approach everybody, even the people we don't really care for or get along with, from that position, we would be amazed by what we would learn from them. Far too often, we view people through the lens of pride and thereby forfeit the riches of the knowledge and experience they offer, settling for the impoverished view from our own limited perspective.

3.   As Peter begins verse 5, he uses the word "likewise." How are younger people to be "like" the elders to whom he has just given instructions to in verses 2-4?

You can tell a lot about a younger person by the way he or she treats those who are older and more seasoned. Likewise, the consideration an older person gives to someone younger reveals a lot about that individual.

Peter is giving very practical instruction here. Elders, yes, you are in a position of authority, but don't go around lording it over others. Your modus operandi should not be rooted in a spirit of pride, just love and serve. And for those who are younger, don't write off those who, as my father says, have "the snows of many winters on their heads." Learn to respect their wisdom and experience. By standing on their shoulders, you will go further faster. What a game changer these types of relationships would be! But they only develop as we put on the right clothing.

4.    What does Peter tell his readers to clothe themselves with in verse 5?

The only way to be clothed in humility as Paul wrote is to "put on the Lord Jesus Christ, and make no provision for the flesh, to gratify its desires" (Romans 13:14).

5.    Read Philippians 2:5-8. How did Paul describe the humility of Jesus?

6.    Look up John 13:3-5. How did Jesus demonstrate humility during His earthly life?

7. What are some ways you can clothe yourself in humility today?

As he finishes up verse 5, Peter gives an ominous warning to those who have a spirit of pride. God will oppose them. The Greek word used for opposed is "antitassō" and means "to range in battle against." Who would want God to be at war with them?

8. Read Acts 12:21-23. What happened when God opposed Herod because of his pride?

As Herod found out, pride is the difference between who you are and who you think you are. The thought of being eaten by worms should be a pretty solid deterrent for pride!

9. Back to 1 Peter 5. Who does Peter say will exalt the person who voluntarily humbles himself or herself? (v.6)

*For every man who promotes himself will be humbled,*
*and every man who learns to be humble will find promotion.*
Matthew 23:12 (PHILLIPS)

Peter then goes on to explain the way we are to humble ourselves before God.

10. In verse 7, what command does Peter give?

What keeps us from being completely dependent on God and giving him all our cares and worries? Pride. The most humble thing we can do is what we read last week in 1 Peter 4:19, "entrust [our] souls to a faithful Creator." Casting our cares upon the Lord means that we trust that He cares for us. Anxiety is actually exalting us above God because what we are saying is that we don't trust Him to take care of our situation. Trust is the essence of humility. It is the confidence that the mighty hand of God is not out to crush us but to care for us.

This week, when your heart rises up in anxiety, choose humility and trust. Humble yourself in confidence and joy as you rest in the hope of God's promise—He cares for you!

No sooner does Peter finish exhorting us to cast our cares upon the Lord, than he switches subjects and yells, "Watch out! There is a lion on the prowl and he will eat you alive if you aren't paying attention!"

The scattered churches who were the original recipients of Peter's letter needed to be very aware that they had an enemy who was going to attack them in the midst of their persecution. He would try to use division, discord, discouragement, and despair to sideline them. He has not updated his approach. As Bob Sorge writes:

> The nature of the enemy's warfare in your life is to cause you to become discouraged and to cast away your confidence. Not that you would necessarily discard your salvation, but you could give up your hope of God's deliverance. The enemy wants to numb you into a coping kind of Christianity that has given up hope of seeing God's resurrection power.[121]

Read 1 Peter 5:8-9.

We have a very real enemy who wants to take us down and take us out. He is relentlessly engaged in schemes and strategies to neutralize us spiritually, rob us of joy, and take away our testimony. John 10:10 is explicit. The enemy's objective is to kill, steal, and destroy. And he is ruthless and opportunistic. He will attack when we least expect it and hit us at our weakest point. He is the original terrorist. So Peter tells us we have to stay on the alert.

1.  What term does Peter use for Satan?

2.  What does the name "adversary" tell us about the devil?

The original word translated "adversary" is a legal term and refers to an opponent in a lawsuit. Make no mistake; an adversary is not a friend or someone to joke around about. The term "devil" comes from the word *diabolos* that means "accuser" or "slanderer". Revelation 12:10 tells us that Satan accuses us "day and night." And he doesn't just accuse us before God; he accuses us to ourselves. He bombards us with self-defeating thoughts that pile on guilt and prompt shame. Remember...He is out to destroy.

He has been prowling around for thousands of years perfecting his temptation techniques.

3.  Read Genesis 3:1-7. What was his strategy with Eve?

The times have changed, but the adversary's scheming ways have not. Notice what the enemy says, "Did God really say that you must not eat any of the fruit of the Garden?" He plants a seed of doubt, raising a question, and Eve answers, "Of course we may eat." But then look at this classic temptation pattern Satan uses. The father of lies (John 8:44) gets Eve to focus, not on the buffet of the thousands of trees from which she could eat delicious fruit, but on the one tree she is not supposed to touch. By asking that one question, the serpent shifts her focus from *bounty* to *want* and covetousness is conceived. She wants what she cannot have. And then she acts on that want.

Elisabeth Elliot explains, "[Spiritual strongholds] begin with a thought. One thought becomes a consideration. A consideration develops into an attitude, which leads then to action. Action repeated becomes a habit, and a habit establishes a 'power base for the enemy,' that is, a stronghold."[122]

Most people who have an affair do so because they fall for the lie that the grass is greener in another part of the garden. They go further down the devil's deceitful rabbit hole by thinking that they can cheat and not get caught or hurt. And then in the aftermath, they find themselves in the rubble of a broken life and wonder what happened. What happened was compromise. The enemy lures us into small compromises, that first look, that lingering thought, that secret desire, that draw us closer and closer to the edge of the cliff of sin. Ephesians 4:27 warns us not to give the enemy a foothold. We can't give him a foothold if we don't get too close. And the further away we stay, the less likely he is to trap us.

4. What are some of the ways the enemy tries to trap you? (Be as specific as possible.)

5. Look up John 12:31; 14:30; and 16:11. What does Jesus call the devil?

The world is the platform from which the adversary launches his assaults. He is the administrator of the fallen world system and he will grab whatever he can and hurl it our way. So we must stay on the alert. Warren Wiersbe writes:

> Satan is a dangerous enemy. He is a serpent who can bite us when we least expect it. He is a destroyer...He has great power and intelligence, and a host of demons who assist him in his attacks against God's people...He is a formidable enemy; we must never joke about him, ignore him, or underestimate his ability. We must "be sober" and have our minds under control when it comes to our conflict with Satan.[123]

We need to recognize the devil's existence and his tactics, but not fear him. As 1 John 4:4 tells us, "greater is He who is in you than he who is in the world." Satan was defeated at Calvary through the shed blood of Christ. As Paul writes in Romans 6:10, "When [Jesus] died, he died once to break the power of sin. But now that he lives, he lives for the glory of God" (Romans 6:10, NLT). The power of sin has been broken and as Romans 16:20 explains, the enemy's final take down is coming. But until that day, we must stand our ground against him.

6. What instruction does Peter give in verse 9?

Kenneth Wuest explains that resist means "to withstand, to be firm against someone else's onset" rather than "to strive against that one." He continues:

> The Christian would do well to remember that he cannot fight the devil. The latter was originally the most powerful and wise angel God created. He still retains much of that power and wisdom as a glance down the pages of history and a look about one today will easily show. While the Christian cannot take the offensive against Satan, yet he can stand his ground in the face of his attacks. Cowardice never wins against Satan, only courage.[124]

One of the greatest motivations to *memorize* God's Word is so that it will be on the tip of our tongue when a *fiery* dart comes our way.

7. Read Ephesians 6:10-18 and James 4:7. What are some ways these verses tell us to resist Satan?

It is important to note that we do not resist in our own power, but by being "firm in [our] faith." Jesus was firm in his faith when Satan came upon Him in the wilderness.

8. Read Matthew 4:1-11. How did Jesus resist the enemy when He was tempted?

Notice that He quoted the verses out loud. One of the greatest motivations to memorize God's Word is so that it will be on the tip of our tongue when a fiery dart comes our way.

9. What are some specific verses that you use to resist the attacks of the enemy?

Prayer is another way we stand firm in our faith when we are being attacked. Jesus taught us to pray, "And do not lead us into temptation but deliver us from evil" (Matthew 6:13). As we read in Ephesians 6:18 we are to "take the sword of the Spirit, praying at all times in the Spirit." Warfare praying is essential to overcoming the adversary.

As Peter wraps up the subject of recognizing and resisting the devil, he reminds his readers that they are not the only ones going through persecution, "the family of believers throughout the world is undergoing the same kind of sufferings" (NIV). Another ruse the devil uses is to make us think that we are the only ones suffering a trial. That is a ploy that can quickly degenerate into a pity party. Peter fortifies his reader's faith by letting them know they are not alone; other believers are going through similar trials. Another way to resist the enemy is to surround ourselves with people who love Jesus. We need to lock arms with other believers for the battle. We cannot do life alone.

And we are not alone. The One who wears the Victor's crown, Jesus Christ, lives in us and is our "hope of glory" (Colossians 1:27). He is our Help. Our Defender. Our Savior. Our Friend. Our indwelling Hope.

> *I'm not afraid of the devil. The devil can handle me – he's got judo I never heard of.*
> *But he can't handle the One to whom I'm joined; he can't handle the One to whom*
> *I'm united; he can't handle the One whose nature dwells in my nature.*[125]
>
> ~ A.W. Tozer

Hallelujah!

# WEEK 9 • DAY FOUR
## I PETER 5:10-11

Whatever your age, you probably have seen the iconic photograph that won a Pulitzer Prize for capturing the horror of war. A 9-year-old girl is running naked down a road in Vietnam with her arms stretched out, screaming in agony. The napalm cloud is swelling in the distance. The date is June 8, 1972. The girl in the picture is Kim Phuc Phan Thi, who became known as the Napalm Girl. The little girl survived the scorching heat of the bomb, but her suffering remained. Kim writes,

> I continued to bear the crippling weight of anger, bitterness, and resentment toward those who caused my suffering—the searing fire that penetrated my body; the ensuing burn baths; the dry and itchy skin; the inability to sweat, which turned my flesh into an oven in Vietnam's sweltering heat. I craved relief that never would come. And yet, despite every last external circumstance that threatened to overtake me—mind, body, and soul—the most agonizing pain I suffered during that season of life dwelled in my heart.

> I was as alone as a person can be. I could not turn to a friend, for nobody wished to befriend me. I was toxic, and everyone knew it. To be near me was to be near hardship. Wise people stayed far away. I was alone, atop a mountain of rage. Why was I made to wear these awful scars? [126]

For ten years, Kim searched for answers. Then on Christmas Eve, a decade after third-degree burns covered 30 percent of her body, she found herself in a church in Saigon listening to a sermon about the gift of Jesus. She realized that it was time to release her pain and exchange it for Jesus. That night she invited Jesus into her heart. In retrospect, Kim shares,

> Those bombs...brought me immeasurable pain. Even now, some 40 years later, I am still receiving treatment for burns that cover my arms, back, and neck. The emotional and spiritual pain was even harder to endure.

> And yet, looking back at the past five decades, I realize that those same bombs that brought so much suffering also brought great healing. Those bombs led me to Christ. [127]

The darkest experience in her life led her to the Light of the World.

Read 1 Peter 5:10-11.

Suffering is a universal language. It is one thing we all have in common. At some point, everyone comes face to face with heartache and pain.

In these two verses, the benediction and doxology for his letter, Peter summarizes what he has been teaching these exiles about suffering.

1.   What preposition does he use at the beginning of verse 10?

"After" refers to the period of time following an event. And what event is Peter referring to? Suffering. In other words, expect it. Don't be caught off guard when it happens. But, then he explains that it will have a limited duration. Suffering will only last for "a little while." It will not continue indefinitely; suffering has an expiration date.

2.   How long will believers experience glory in Christ?

3.   How does Peter's reminder about the length of suffering contrasted with the length of glory encourage a believer who is going through a trial?

So we're not giving up. How could we! Even though on the outside it often looks like things are falling apart on us, on the inside, where God is making new life, not a day goes by without His unfolding grace. These hard times are small potatoes compared to the coming good times, the lavish celebration prepared for us. There's far more here than meets the eye. The things we see now are here today, gone tomorrow. But the things we can't see now will last forever.

2 Corinthians 4:16-18 (MSG)

The central statement in verse 10 is the reference Peter makes to God. He calls Him, "the God of all grace." This is the only time in the Bible this title is used. Peter encourages these persecuted believers by emphasizing the character of God. Noting that He is not just the God of grace but "the God of *all* grace," Peter tells them that they have hope in the One who is the definitive source and sole distributor of grace. What is grace? It is undeserved favor. We need grace because we are sinners who are in constant need of forgiveness. We need grace because we are saints who have problems and struggles that we cannot manage on our own. Grace is also the desire and the ability to do the will of God; both are necessary ingredients during times of suffering.

Through many dangers, toils, and snares,
I have already come;
Tis grace hath brought me safe this far,
And grace will lead me home.[128]

4.   What four words does Peter use to describe God's purpose for suffering?

"Perfect" means to equip, repair, or render complete. It is the same word that was used to describe Peter "mending" his nets in Matthew 4:21. "Confirm" means to fix, set fast, or strengthen. This Greek word, for "Strengthen" occurs only this one time in the Bible and means just that. God will give us strength to withstand the demands of life. "Establish" means to lay the foundation. Jesus used the same word in Matthew 7:25 to describe the house built upon the rock that withstood the storm.

John Ortberg writes,

> If you ask people who don't believe in God why they don't, the number one reason is suffering. If you ask people who believe in God when they grew most spiritually, the number one reason is suffering.[129]

When an unbeliever experiences suffering, he or she loses hope. When a believer suffers, if he or she responds correctly, hope increases.

5.  Read Romans 5:3-4. What does Paul say that suffering will produce?

Our problems, our trials, our suffering is never wasted. God is using them to make us who we are called to be in Christ.

As Peter reaches verse 11, you can hear the rallying cry with which he declares his worship—"To Him be dominion forever and ever. Amen."

Dominion is the presence, significance, and power of strength. Peter is saying that we should praise God for what He has done and will do. Eugene Peterson translates 1 Peter 5:10-11:

> The suffering won't last forever. It won't be long before this generous God who has great plans for us in Christ—eternal and glorious plans they are!—will have you put together and on your feet for good. He gets the last word; yes, He does. (MSG)

He has the final word. Every. Time. As Kim Phuc Phan Thi recounts:

> Nearly half a century has passed since I found myself running—frightened, naked, and in pain—down that road in Vietnam. I will never forget the horrors of that day—the bombs, the fire, the shrieks, the fear. Nor will I forget the years of trial and torment that followed. But when I think about how far I have come—the freedom and peace that comes from faith in Jesus—I realize there is nothing greater or more powerful than the love of our blessed Savior.
>
> My faith in Jesus has enabled me to forgive those who have hurt and scarred me. It has enabled me to pray for my enemies rather than curse them. And it has enabled me not just to tolerate them but truly to love them.

I will forever bear the scars of that day, and that picture will always serve as a reminder of the unspeakable evil of which humanity is capable. That picture defined my life. In the end, it gave me a mission, a ministry, a cause.

Today, I thank God for that picture. Today, I thank God for everything—even for that road. Especially for that road.[130]

*To Him be dominion forever and ever. Amen.*

Abigail Adams, the wife of John Adams, the second U.S. president, and the mother of John Quincy Adams, the sixth president, was a woman of great faith and insight. On January 19, 1780, she wrote a wartime letter to her son, John Quincy, who was travelling abroad with his father, a United States diplomat at the time. Abigail urged her ten-year-old son to take full advantage of this incredible opportunity. She challenged him to gain wisdom and experience growth throughout his time abroad, encouraging him to take his first steps to becoming a leader. The following is an excerpt from her letter:

> These are times in which a genius would wish to live. It is not in the still calm of life, or the repose of a pacific station, that great characters are formed...The habits of a vigorous mind are formed in contending with difficulties. Great necessities call out great virtues. When a mind is raised, and animated by scenes that engage the heart, then those qualities which would otherwise lay dormant, wake into life, and form the character of the hero and the statesman.[131]

Adams' words to her son are similar to Peter's message to the hurting people, the scattered church, who were the original recipients of his letter and to the *ecclesia*, those who have answered the bidding of Jesus to be the "called out ones," and have for centuries functioned as a touch point between Heaven and earth, where the power of the cross redeems the lost and the hope of the resurrection transforms the saved into the likeness of Christ.

Are you walking through difficulty? Enduring a period of suffering? *Great necessities call out great virtues.* Peter tells us these are the times we are to "greatly rejoice with joy inexpressible and full of glory" (1:8), and "fervently love one another from the heart" (1:22), "putting aside all malice and all deceit and hypocrisy and envy and all slander" (2:1), silencing those who hurl "accusations against you" (2:15 NLT), "casting all your anxiety on Him, because He cares for you" (5:7).

*These are times in which a genius would wish to live. The times when qualities which would otherwise lay dormant, wake into life.* The times when we are transformed into the character of Christ. These are the times that call for Outrageous Hope and Extravagant Joy!

Yesterday we read Peter's benediction (*good word*) in 1 Peter 5:10 and his doxology (*hymn of praise*) in verse 11. We might think that the "Amen" would signal the end of the letter, but not surprisingly, Peter has just a couple of more things to say after the Amen.

Read 1 Peter 5:12-14.

1.  Who assisted Peter in the writing of the letter? (v.12)

Peter dictated the letter to Silas (Silvanus) up until 5:12, and then Peter takes the pen into his own hand and adds his final words. Besides the content of verses 12-14, evidence that Peter wrote this part is seen in the change to a simpler grammar and vocabulary in the Greek text.

Who is Silas, this faithful brother? Silas is first mentioned in Acts 15:22 when he is selected by the elders to accompany Paul and Barnabas to Antioch following the Jerusalem Council. But, he is not just the guy who travels with Paul to carry his suitcases; he carried the gospel. After Paul and Barnabas disagreed over Mark's involvement in the ministry, Silas is the one who replaced Barnabas on Paul's missionary journeys. In Acts 16:25-30, it is Silas who is singing at midnight with Paul in the Philippian jail. Paul mentions Silas in the salutations of both of his letters to the Thessalonians. This "faithful brother" also ministered with Timothy at Corinth (2 Corinthians 1:19). And now we find that he has been loyally serving with Peter in Rome, among other things, functioning as a scribe. Chuck Swindoll notes, "God gives Peter the message, Silas writes it down, and the Spirit of God ignites it."[132]

Silas was a true-blue, devoted leader who linked arms with both Paul and Peter in their ministries. We all need a Silas in our lives, someone who will resolutely stand with us, and we need to be a Silas, a loyal stalwart, to someone else.

2.  Peter summarizes the reason he wrote the letter in verse 12. What is it?

Peter was the apostle of hope. And that is the message of his letter—we have a living hope in the living Christ. We, like the exiles scattered across the Roman Empire, may face difficulty and an uncertain future, but we can stand fast in the grace of God. The word grace shows up in every chapter of 1 Peter. Dallas Willard defines grace as "God's action in our lives to accomplish what we cannot accomplish on our own."[133]

Think about the words of the hymn writer:

*Dressed in His righteousness alone,*
*faultless to stand before the throne.*[134]
*~ Edward Mote*

By grace our weakness morphs into strength and our trials turn into triumphs. In the cold face of suffering, grace is a generous, limitless gift from God even though we don't even deserve the wrapping paper it comes in.

By what means does He swap our closet full of sin and brokenness for a faultless wardrobe of righteousness? Grace. By grace we are saved. By grace our weakness morphs into strength and our trials turn into triumphs. In the cold face of suffering, grace is a generous, limitless gift from God even though we don't even deserve the wrapping paper it comes in. And as they say, we can take that to the bank. Or as Peter says, we can "stand firm in it" while we are waiting for our current difficulty to become yesterday's news.

Now for a FAQ (Frequently Asked Question)...who is the "she" Peter refers to in verse 13? And the answer is, we don't exactly know. However, most theologians believe it is a broad reference to the church at Rome. Since the Roman Empire was the Jews' worst enemy, Peter would probably have used the pseudonym of Babylon, a city known for its debauchery, to refer to the location of the church at Rome as he sends his final greetings.

3.  Who else does Peter send greetings from?

John Mark was well known by the recipients of Peter's letter. He was Barnabas' cousin and Peter considered him to be like "a son". Peter was Mark's main source of information for his Gospel, was with him earlier in Rome (Colossians 4:10), and was with him when he wrote this letter.

4.  What are the closing words of the old fisherman's letter?

In the early church, Christians would kiss each other on the cheek and say, "Peace be with you" or simply just the Hebrew word for peace, "Shalom". Augustine said that when Christians met, "they communicated their inward peace by the outward peace."[135] It was a demonstration of unity, love, and peace. Peter opens (1:2) and closes (5:13) his letter with a blessing of peace, invoking God's peace into the lives of his readers.

As Peter puts the cap on his pen, his resounding message hangs thick in the air. Regardless of what comes next, deliverance or death, joy or pain, they have a "living hope" that will carry them through. And their story is far from over.

*The Chronicles of Narnia,* a children's series written by C.S. Lewis, invites us into the lives of Peter, Susan, Edmund, Lucy, Caspian, Eustace, Jill, and others to experience the challenges they face in the fantasy land of Narnia. Aslan, the lion, is the Christ figure around which every Narnian adventure is centered. As the last book draws to a close, Aslan lifts the veil to reveal to the children what has, in reality, taken place.

> 'There was a real railway accident,' said Aslan softly. 'Your father and mother and all of you are — as you used to call it in the Shadowlands — dead. The term is over: the holidays have begun. The dream is ended: this is the morning'. And as He spoke He no longer looked to them like a lion; but the things that began to happen after that were so great and beautiful that I cannot write them. And for us this is the end of all the stories, and we can most truly say that they all lived happily ever after. But for them it was only the beginning of the real story. All their life in this world and all their adventures in Narnia had *only been the cover and the title page*: now at last they were beginning Chapter One of the Great Story which no one on earth has read; which goes on forever; in which every chapter is better than the one before.[136]

For all believers, whether first century or twenty-first century readers of Peter's letter, the story of our lives only gets better after we get past the "cover and the title page" into the eternal forever of Chapter One. But don't waste *your time in the meantime*. Ask God to show you what to do in your life and the lives of others – while you wait. And then do it with Outrageous Hope and Extravagant Joy!

# ⇒ HOW TO BECOME A CHRISTIAN ⇐

Dear one, has there ever been a time that you have given your heart to the Lord? Do you have the assurance that if you were to die right now, you would go straight to heaven to spend all eternity in the presence of the Lord Jesus Christ and all His followers? If not, please let me share with you how you can be saved.

**Admit Your Sin**

First, you must understand that you are a sinner. The Bible says, *All have sinned and fall short of the glory of God* (Rom. 3:23). In Romans 6:23 the Bible says, *For the wages of sin is death.* That means that sin has separated us from a Holy God and we are under the sentence of eternal death and separation from God.

**Abandon Self-Effort**

Secondly, you must understand that you cannot save yourself by your own efforts. The Bible is very clear that it is *not by works of righteousness which we have done, but according to His mercy He saved us* (Titus 3:5). Again, in Ephesians 2:8-9 the Bible says, *For by grace you have been saved through faith; and that not of yourselves, it is the gift of God; not as a result of works, that no one should boast.*

**Acknowledge Christ's Payment**

Thirdly, you must believe that Jesus Christ, the Son of God, died for your sins. The Bible says, *God demonstrates His own love toward us, in that while we were yet sinners, Christ died for us* (Rom. 5:8). That means He died a sacrificial death in your place. Your sin debt has been paid by the blood of Jesus Christ, which *cleanses us from all sin* (I John 1:7).

**Accept Him as Savior**

Fourthly, you must put your faith in Jesus Christ and Him alone for your salvation. The blood of Christ does you no good until you receive Him by faith. The Bible says, *Believe on the Lord Jesus Christ, and you shall be saved* (Acts 16:31).

Has there been a time in your life that you have taken this all-important step of faith? If not, I urge you to do it right now. Jesus Christ is the only way to heaven. He said, *"I am the way, the truth, and the life; no man comes unto the Father, but by Me"* (John 14:16).

Would you like to become a Christian? Would you like to invite Jesus Christ to come into your heart today? Read over this prayer and if it expresses the desire of your heart, you may ask Him into your heart to take away your sin, fill you with His Spirit, and take you home to heaven when you die. If this is your intention, pray this prayer.

*"Oh God, I'm a sinner. I am lost and I need to be saved. I know I cannot save myself, so right now, once and for all, I trust You to save me. Come into my heart, forgive my sin, and make me Your child. I give you my life. I will live for You as You give me Your strength. Amen"*

If you will make this your heartfelt prayer, God will hear and save you! Jesus has promised that He will never leave nor forsake anyone who comes to Him in faith. In John 6:37 He said, *"The One who comes to Me I will certainly not cast out."*

Welcome to the family!

# END NOTES

**Introduction**

1.  Piper, J. (2004). *Seeing and Savoring Christ*, p. 72. Wheaton, IL: Crossway Books.

2.  Boustany, N. (April 29, 2005). As Ukraine Watched the Party Line, She Took the Truth Into Her Hands. *The Washington Post*. Retrieved from http://www.washingtonpost.com/wp-dyn/content/article /2005/04/28/ AR2005042801696.html.

3.  Yancey, P. (2010). *What Good is God?*, p. 185. New York, NY: FaithWords Publishing.

4.  Swindoll, C. (1996). *Hope Again,* p. 5. Dallas, TX: Word Publishing.

5.  Wiersbe, W. *Be Hopeful*, p. 11. Colorado Springs, CO: Victor Books.

**Week 1**

6.  Wiersbe, W. (1989). *The Bible Exposition Commentary*, p. 390. Wheaton, IL: SP Publications, Inc.

7.  Schreiner, T. (2003). *The New American Commentary, 1, 2 Peter, Jude*, p. 49. Nashville, TN: Broadman & Holman Publishers.

8.  Raymer, R. M. (1985). 1 Peter. In J. F. Walvoord & R. B. Zuck (Eds.), *The Bible Knowledge Commentary: An Exposition of the Scriptures Volume 2*, p. 839. Wheaton, IL: Victor Books.

9.  Wiersbe, W. (1989). *The Bible Exposition Commentary*, p. 391-392. Wheaton, IL: SP Publications, Inc.

10. Wiersbe, W. (1989). *The Bible Exposition Commentary*, p. 392. Wheaton, IL: SP Publications, Inc.

11. *The ESV Study Bible*, p. 2525-2526. (2008). Wheaton, IL: Crossway.

12. Wiersbe, W. (1989). *The Bible Exposition Commentary*, p. 393. Wheaton, IL: SP Publications, Inc.

13. Hughes, C. (May 6, 2018) My Declaration in My Darkest Hour. *Desiring God*. Retrieved from https://www.desiringgod.org/articles/my-declaration-in-my-darkest-hour

14. Zodhiates, S., ed. (1996). *Hebrew Greek Key Word Study Bible*, p. 1669. Chattanooga, TN: AMG International, Inc.

15. Zodhiates, S., ed. (1996). *Hebrew Greek Key Word Study Bible*, p. 1669. Chattanooga, TN: AMG International, Inc.

16. Zodhiates, S., ed. (1996). *Hebrew Greek Key Word Study Bible*, p. 1669-1670. Chattanooga, TN: AMG International, Inc.

17. *The ESV Study Bible*, p. 23. (2008). Wheaton, IL: Crossway.

18. Schreiner, T. (2003). *The New American Commentary: 1, 2 Peter, Jude*, p. 76. Nashville, TN: Broadman & Holman Publishers.

**Week 2**

19. Batterson, M. (2013). *All In*, p. 17. Grand Rapids, MI: Zondervan.

20. Alcorn, R. (2005). *Happiness*, p. 361. Carol Stream, IL: Tyndale House Publishers, Inc.

21. Wiersbe, W. (1989) *Bible Exposition Commentary*, p. 395. Wheaton, IL: SP Publications, Inc.

22. Wuest, K. (1961). *The New Testament: An Expanded Translation*, p. 550. Grand Rapids, MI: William B. Eerdmans Publishing Company.

23. Holman Bible Dictionary (n.d.).Retrieved from https://www.studylight.org/dictionaries/hbd/f/future-hope.html

24. Willard, D. (2006). *The Great Omission*, p. 30. New York, NY: HarperCollins Publishers, Inc.

25. Meyer, F.B. (1993). *Tried by Fire,* p. 51. Fort Washington, PA: Christian Literature Crusade.

26. Bridges, J. (1978). *The Pursuit of Holiness,* p. 64. Colorado Springs, CO: NavPress.

27. Alcorn, R. (2015). *Happiness,* p. 357. Carol Stream, IL: Tyndale House Publishers.

28. Alcorn, R. (2015). *Happiness*, p. 358. Carol Stream, IL: Tyndale House Publishers.

29. Moral and ethical wholeness or perfection; freedom from moral evil. (2014). *Nelson's Bible Dictionary*. Nashville, TN: Thomas Nelson Incorporated.

30. Lewis, C.S. (2011). *Letters to An American Lady*, p. 11. Grand Rapids, MI: WM. B. Eerdman's Publishing.

31. Wiersbe, W. (1982). *Be Hopeful,* p. 51. Colorado Springs, CO: David C. Cook.

32. Willard, D. (1998). *The Divine Conspiracy*, p. 301. New York, NY: HarperCollins Publishers, Inc.

33. Willard, D. (2006). *The Great Omission*, p. 11. New York, NY: HarperCollins Publishers, Inc.

34. Willard, D. (1998). *The Divine Conspiracy*, p. 301. New York, NY: HarperCollins Publishers, Inc.

**Week 3**

35. Willard, D. (1998). *The Divine Conspiracy*, p. 335. New York, NY: HarperCollins Publishers, Inc.

36. Henry, M. (1994). *Matthew Henry's Commentary on the Whole Bible: Complete and Unabridged in One Volume,* p. 2426. Peabody: Hendrickson.

37. MacArthur, J. F., Jr. (2004). *1 Peter*, p. 137. Chicago: Moody Publishers.

**Week 4**

38. Elliot, E. (1976). *Let Me Be a Woman*, p. 43. Carol Stream, IL: Tyndale House.

39. Whatever. (n.d.). *Merriam-Webster Dictionary.* Retrieved from https://www.merriam-webster.com/dictionary/whatever

40. *Life Application Study Bible, New Living Translation,* p. 2787. (2007). Carol Stream, IL: Tyndale House Publishers, Inc.

41. Cole, Steven J. (2012). The Government and You. *Bible.Org.* Retrieved from https://bible.org/seriespage/lesson-88-government-and-you-romans-131-7.

42. Barclay, William. (1961). *The Letters of James and Peter*, p. 240. Louisville, KY: Westminster John Knox Press.

43. McGee, J. Vernon. (1983). *Thru the Bible with J. Vernon McGee,* p. 694. Nashville, TN: Thomas Nelson Publishers.

44. Krell, Keith R. (2010). *The Freedom of Slavery.* Retrieved from https://bible.org/seriespage/14-freedom-slavery-romans-615-23#P21_7618

45. Piper, John. (May 29, 1994). Slaves of God: Free From All to Honor All. *Desiring God.* Retrieved from https://www.desiringgod.org/messages/slaves-of-god-free-from-all-to-honor-al

46. Carmichael, Amy. (2003). *If*, p. 13. Fort Washington, PA: CLC Publications.

47. Sproul, R.C. (2018). Love Your Brothers. *Ligonier Ministries.* Retrieved from https://www.ligonier.org/learn/devotionals/love-your-brothers/

48. Piper, John. (January 12, 2016). Fear God, Not the Government. *Desiring God.* Retrieved from https://www.desiringgod.org/labs/fear-god-not-the-government

49. *Life Application Study Bible*, New Living Translation, p. 2788 (2007). Carol Stream, IL: Tyndale House Publishers, Inc.

50. Deffinbaugh, Robert L. (July 3, 2004). The Submission of Slaves to Masters. *Bible.Org.* https://bible.org/seriespage/submission-slaves-masters-1-peter-218-25#P1630_465473

51. Wolgemuth, Nancy DeMoss. How to Endure Suffering. *Revive our Hearts.* Retrieved from https://www.reviveourhearts.com/articles/how-to-endure-suffering/

52. Nee, W. (2014). *Release of the Spirit*, p. 95. New York, NY: Christian Fellowship Publishers, Inc.

53. Sproul, R.C. (2018). Holy Truth. *Ligonier*. https://www.ligonier.org/learn/devotionals/holy-truth/

54. *The Spurgeon Study Bible, CSB,* p. 1670. (2017). Nashville, TN: Holman Bible Publishers.

55. Grant, Natalie. (2010). *Song to the King.* Nat-In-The-Hat-Music.

56. Sproul, R.C. (2018). Shepherd and Overseer. *Ligonier*. Retrieved from https://www.ligonier.org/learn/devotionals/shepherd-

**Week 5**

57. *Ann Voskamp*. Retrieved from http://annvoskamp.com/sticky-notes-signup/

58. Deffinbaugh, Robert L. (July 3, 2004). A Word to Wives. Bible.Org. Retrieved from https://bible.org/seriespage/13-word-wives-1-peter-31-6

59. Cole, Steven J. (August 2, 2013). Living With a Difficult Husband. *Bible.Org.* Retrieved from https://bible.org/seriespage/lesson-14-living-difficult-husband-1-peter-31-6

60. Chapman, Gary. (2010). How To Truly Love Your Spouse. *Focus on the Family*. Retrieved from https://www.focusonthefamily.com/marriage/ strengthening-your-marriage/how-to-truly-love-your-spouse

61. Fulk, Heidi Jo. (March 9, 2017). The Pursuit of Quiet. *Revive Our Hearts.* Retrieved from https://www.reviveourhearts.com/true-woman/blog/pursuit-quiet/

62. Wagner, Kimberly. Characteristics of a Meek and Quiet Spirit. *Revive Our Hearts.* Retrieved from https://www.reviveourhearts.com/ articles/characteristics-meek-and-quiet-spirit/

63. *Life Application Study Bible, New Living Translation,* p. 2789. (2007). Carol Stream, IL: Tyndale House Publishers, Inc.

64. McGee, J. Vernon. (1983). *Thru the Bible with J. Vernon McGee,* p. 699. Nashville, TN: Thomas Nelson Publishers.

65. McGee, J. Vernon. (1983). *Thru the Bible with J. Vernon McGee,* p. 699. Nashville, TN: Thomas Nelson Publishers.

66. *Life Application Study Bible, New Living Translation,* p. 2790. (2007). Carol Stream, IL: Tyndale House Publishers, Inc.

67. Carmichael, Amy. (2003). *If*, p. 35. Fort Washington, PA: CLC Publications.

68. Carmichael, Amy. (2003). *If*, p. 35. Fort Washington, PA: CLC Publications.

69. McGee, J. Vernon. (1983). *Thru the Bible with J. Vernon McGee,* p. 700. Nashville, TN: Thomas Nelson Publishers.

**Week 6**

70. Thomas, I. (1993). *If I Perish, I Perish*, p. 96. Estes Park, CO: Torchbearer Publications.

71. Wheaton, D.H. (1994). 1 Peter. In D. A. Carson, R. T. France, J. A. Motyer, & G. J. Wenham (Eds.), New *Bible Commentary: 21st Century Edition*, p. 1379. Leicester, England; Downers Grove, IL: Inter-Varsity Press.

72. Taylor, J. (December 7, 2016). A Woman of Whom the World Was Not Worthy: Helen Roseveare. *The Gospel Coalition*. Retrieved from https://www.thegospelcoalition.org/blogs/justin-taylor/a-woman-of-whom-the world-was-not-worthy-helen-roseveare-1925-2016/

73. Taylor J. (December 7, 2016). A Woman of whom the World Was Not Worthy: Helen Roseveare. *The Gospel Coalition*. Retrieved from https://www.thegospelcoalition.org/blogs/justin-taylor/a-woman-of-whom-the world-was-not-worthy-helen-roseveare-1925-2016/

74. Zodhiates, S., ed. (1996). *Hebrew Greek Key Word Study Bible*, p. 2049. Chattanooga, TN: AMG International, Inc.

75. Zodhiates, S., ed. (1996). *Hebrew Greek Key Word Study Bible*, p. 1572. Chattanooga, TN: AMG International, Inc.

76. Ludy, L. (May 26, 2016) The Power of Suffering Well for Christ. *Revive Our Hearts*. Retrieved from https://www.reviveourhearts.com/true-woman/blog/esther-ahn-kim-power-suffering-well-christ/.

77. Schreiner, T. (2003). *The New American Commentary, 1, 2 Peter, Jude*, p. 174. Nashville, TN: Broadman & Holman Publishers.

78. Ludy, L. (May 26, 2016) The Power of Suffering Well for Christ. *Revive Our Hearts*. Retrieved from https://www.reviveourhearts.com/true-woman/blog/esther-ahn-kim-power-suffering-well-christ/.

79. Sharp, M. (2015). *Living in Truth*, p. 19. Nashville, TN: LifeWay Press.

80. Banerjee, N. (June 24, 2008). Survey Shows U. S. Religious Tolerance. *New York Times*. Retrieved from https://www.nytimes.com/2008/06/24/us/ 24religion.html

81. Sharp, M. (2015). *Living in Truth*, p. 97. Nashville, TN: LifeWay Press.

82. Sharp, M. (2015). *Living in Truth*, p. 35. Nashville, TN: LifeWay Press.

83. Zodhiates, S., ed. (1996). *Hebrew Greek Key Word Study Bible*, p. 1675. Chattanooga, TN: AMG International, Inc.

84. Wiersbe, W. (1989). *The Bible Exposition Commentary*, p. 414. Wheaton, IL: SP Publications, Inc.

85. Doyle, T. (2015). *Killing Christians*, p. 99. Nashville, TN: W Publishing Group.

86. Doyle, T. (2015). *Killing Christians*, p. 101. Nashville, TN: W Publishing Group.

87. Wheaton, D.H. (1994). 1 Peter. In D. A. Carson, R. T. France, J. A. Motyer, & G. J. Wenham (Eds.), *New Bible Commentary: 21st Century Edition*, p. 1379. Leicester, England; Downers Grove, IL: Inter-Varsity Press.

88. Schreiner, T. (2003). *The New American Commentary: 1, 2 Peter, Jude,* p. 184. Nashville, TN: Broadman & Holman Publishers.

89. *The Woman's Study Bible* (1995). p. 2070. Nashville TN: Thomas Nelson Publishers.

90. Raymer, R.M. (1985). 1 Peter. In J. F. Walvoord & R. B. Zuck (Eds.), *The Bible Knowledge Commentary: An Exposition of the Scriptures* (Vol. 2, p. 852). Wheaton, IL: Victor Books.

91. Mote, E. (1991). The Solid Rock, p. 406. Nashville, TN: Broadman & Holman Publishers.

**Week 7**

92. Meyers, F.B. *The Works of F.B. Meyers, Volume 2.* Loc. 29359. Kindle Edition.

93. Meyers, F.B. *The Works of F.B. Meyers, Volume 2.* Loc. 29391. Kindle Edition.

94. Willard, D. (1998). *The Divine Conspiracy*, p. 356. New York, NY: Harper Collins Publishers.

95. *Tyndale New Testament Commentary, The First Epistle General of Peter*. (1959). p. 146. Carol Stream, IL: Tyndale Press.

96. Willard, D. (1998). *The Divine Conspiracy*, p. 348. New York, NY: HarperCollins Publishers.

97. *Tyndale New Testament Commentary, The First Epistle General of Peter*. (1959). p. 154. Carol Stream, IL: Tyndale Press.

98. *The Economist*. (June 16, 2015). Retrieved from https://www.economist. com /democracy-in-america/2018/06/15/americas-rising-suicide-rate

99. Fox, M. (May 11, 2018). Major Depression on the Rise for Everyone, New Data Shows. *NBC News*. Retrieved from https://www.nbcnews.com/health/health-news/major-depression-rise-among everyone-new-data-shows-n873146

100. Hoang, B., Johnson, K. (2016). *The Justice Calling: Where Passion Meets Perseverance*, p. 17. Grand Rapids, MI: Brazos Press.

101. Willis, D., Clements, B. (2017). *The Simplest Way to Change the World*, p. 72. Chicago, IL: Moody Publishers.

102. Butterfield, R. (2018). *The Gospel Comes with a House Key,* p. Loc.402. Wheaton, IL: Crossway.

103. Hannon, A. (2017). *Love, Welcome, Serve*, p. 11. New York, NY: Hachette Book Group, Inc.

104. Hannon, A. (2017). *Love, Welcome, Serve*, p. 11. New York, NY: Hachette Book Group, Inc.

105. Hill, A. (2018). *Missional Motherhood*. Retrieved from URL. http://missionalmotherhood.com/hospitality/hospitality-that-speaks/

**Week 8**

106. Sprugeon, C. (1855). *Sermon No. 35, Pulpit Volume 1*. New Park Street.

107. Swindoll, C. R. (2010). *Insights on James and 1 & 2 Peter,* p. 227. Grand Rapids, MI: Zondervan.

108. Stockdale, J. (2008). *Joy in the Journey,* p. 95. Garland, TX: Crosshouse  Publishing.

109. Stockdale, J. (2008). *Joy in the Journey,* p. 95. Garland, TX: Crosshouse Publishing.

110. MacArthur, J. F., Jr. (2001). *Philippians,* p. 95. Chicago, IL: Moody Press.

111. Henry, M. (1994). *Matthew Henry's Commentary on the Whole Bible: Complete and Unabridged in One Volume,* p. 2432. Peabody: Hendrickson.

112. Wuest, K. S. (1997). *Wuest's Word Studies from the Greek New Testament: For the English Reader* (Vol. 11), p. 121. Grand Rapids: Eerdmans.

**Week 9**

113. Keller, T. (2017). *Daily Keller.* Retrieved from http://dailykeller.com/category/suffering/

114. Keller, P. (1970). *A Shepherd Looks at Psalm 23,* pp. 20-21.  Grand Rapids, MI: Zondervan Publishing.

115. Swindoll, C. (1996). *Hope Again*, p. 227. Dallas, TX: Word Publishing.

116. Piper, J. (2016). *Desiring God.* Retrieved from https://www.desiringgod.org/messages/the-inexplicable-life

117. Piper, J. (2012). *Future Grace*, p. 83. New York, NY: Waterbrook Multnomah.

118. Murray, A. (2017). *Humility*, preface. Kindle edition. Public domain.

119. Warren, R. (2012). *The Purpose Driven Life,* p. 262. Grand Rapids, MI: Zondervan Publishing.

120. Carlyle, T. (n.d.). *AZ Quotes*. Retrieved from http://www.azquotes.com/quote/388718

121. Sorge, B. (2011). *Glory: When Heaven Invades Earth,* p. 75. Kansas City, MO: Oasis House.

122. Elliot, E. (1982). *Discipline: Glad Surrender,* p. 66. Grand Rapids, MI: Baker Publishing.

123. Wiersbe, W. (1982). *Be Hopeful*, p. 138. Colorado Springs, CO: Victor Books.

124. Wuest, K. S. (1997). *Wuest's Word Studies from the Greek New Testament: For the English Reader,* Vol. 11, p. 130. Grand Rapids, MI: Eerdmans.

125. Tozer, A.W. (2018). *The Quotable Tozer, ebook.* Bloomington, MN: Bethany House Publishers.

126. Thi, K.P.P. (April 20, 2018). These Bombs Led Me to Christ. *Christianity Today.* Retrieved from https://www.christianitytoday.com/ct/2018/may/napalm-girl-kim-phuc-phan-thi-fire-road.html

127. Thi, K.P.P. (April 20, 2018). These Bombs Led Me to Christ. *Christianity Today.* Retrieved from https://www.christianitytoday.com/ct/2018/may/napalm-girl-kim-phuc-phan-thi-fire-road.html

128. Newton, J. (1991). Amazing Grace. *The Baptist Hymnal*, p. 330. Nashville, TN: Broadman and Holman Publishers.

129. Ortberg, J. (2014). *Soul Keeping: Caring for the Most Important Part of You,* p. 179. Grand Rapids, MI: Zondervan Publishing.

130. Thi, K.P.P. (April 20, 2018). These Bombs Led Me to Christ. *Christianity Today.* Retrieved from https://www.christianitytoday.com/ct/2018/may/napalm-girl-kim-phuc-phan-thi-fire-road.html

131. Adams, A. (n.d.). *Adams Papers Digital Edition*. Retrieved from http://www.masshist.org/publications/adams-papers/view?id=ADMS-04-03- 02-0207

132. Swindoll, C. (1996). *Hope Again*, p. 271. Dallas, TX: Word Publishing.

133. Willard, D. (1998). *The Divine Conspiracy: Rediscovering Our Hidden Life In God,* p. 88. New York, NY: Harper Collins Publishers.

134. Mote, E. (1991). The Solid Rock. *The Baptist Hymnal*, p. 406. Nashville, TN: Broadman and Holman Publishers.

135. Smith, W. (1880). *A Dictionary of Christian Antiquities*, Vol. 2, p. 904. Hartford, CO: J.B. Burr Publishing.

136. Lewis, C.S. (1984). *The Last Battle*, p. 228. New York: NY: Harper Collins Publishers.